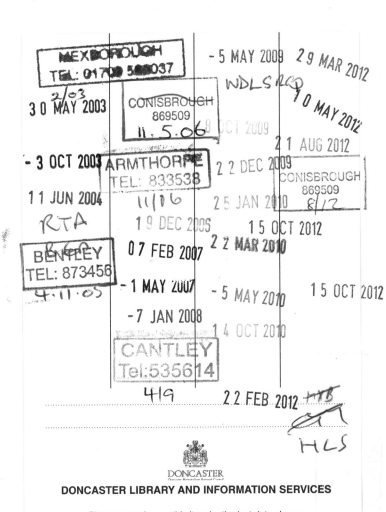

IT WAS LIKE THIS . . .

IT WAS LIKE THIS . . .

Mabel Winifred Redwood

ISIS
LARGE PRINT
Oxford

First published in Great Britain 2001
by Barbara Anslow

Published in Large Print 2002 by ISIS Publishing Ltd,
7 Centremead, Osney Mead, Oxford OX2 0ES
by arrangement with Barbara Anslow

British Library Cataloguing in Publication Data
Redwood, Mabel Winifred, 1895–1975
   It was like this.... – Large print ed. –
(ISIS reminiscence series)
1. Redwood, Mabel Winifred, 1895–1975
2. Prisoners of war – Great Britain – Biography
3. Prisoners of war – China – Hong Kong – Biography
4. World War, 1939–1945 – Prisoners and prisons,
Japanese
5. Large type books
I. Title
940.5'47252'092

ISBN 0–7531–9808–8 (hb)
ISBN 0–7531–9809–6 (pb)

Printed and bound by Antony Rowe, Chippenham

Contents

1 In Kent and Scotland 1

2 Going to Hong Kong (twice) 35

3 Being Evacuees 62

4 Invaded and Besieged 75

5 When We Came to Our Cuttings Down .. 132

6 Afterwards 231

7 Poems and Letters 259

CHAPTER
ONE

In Kent and Scotland

"Well, who's going to hang up their stockings tonight?" whispered Connie as we crawled into our cold camp beds in the darkness. Most of us were still wearing our grey Auxiliary Nursing Services uniforms, the niceties of washing and undressing at bedtime being things of the past in Hong Kong this Christmas Eve 1941.

The Japanese had attacked the colony three weeks earlier and were now swarming all over the island. Intermittent shellfire had become a familiar sound, together with that of planes roaring overhead and the thud of bombs. Bullets from nearby snipers' rifles made you think twice before you ventured to the lavatories which were across the open yard.

Connie's joke helped, for we felt the situation could hardly have been grimmer. We were a group of about twenty-four European women and Connie, an irrepressible Australian, helping to run a war-time casualty clearing hospital set up in the Hong Kong Jockey Club building in Happy Valley. Our patients were Chinese and few spoke English. The military situation made it impossible for us to return to our homes after ward duty so we were compelled to live on the job. The water supply had failed; we were unable to wash either ourselves or the patients. Bedpans could not be emptied or cleaned, rice could not be cooked, and all food was scarce. The military post next door to our hospital (in another section of the Jockey Club) had been abandoned. We appeared to be cut off from our own people; our last visitor — a Methodist minister — had told us that there was heavy fighting some miles from us, but that our forces were holding the enemy. The oil installations about a mile beyond our position were in flames, as was a row of houses on a rise just opposite the Jockey Club. There was no telephone communication.

That afternoon trench mortars had been fired into our hospital, though by a miracle no one was hit. The patients were accommodated in beds in the betting hall which had no doors, only large entrances open to the weather (and the war). These entrances had been partially sandbagged but some of the mortars cleared the sandbags and exploded on the concrete floor within.

Lack of manpower and the constant risk of coming under fire meant that bodies of dead patients were piling up in the garages outside and spreading putrefaction. We were all separated from our families and fearful for their ordeals in some other corner of the Colony. Hungry, weary, dirty, frightened and apprehensive, we came off the day duty and tried to settle for the night.

It was only when Connie spoke that we remembered it was Christmas Eve. For a few minutes there was an exchange of banter on the subject, then, out of sheer exhaustion, we slept.

Machine-gun fire woke us up suddenly. It was alarmingly near. Everyone sat up. The firing continued and seemed to be getting nearer. We began to see the reflection of the flashes in the high windows which faced the road; there were bursts of firing on the other side of us and we realised with horror that fighting was going on all round us.

Then came a change in the tempo of the firing, and it gradually dawned on us that the Japanese were fighting their way towards us, and our men were being driven back towards the city, so here we were, helpless, between the lines, right in the path of the advancing enemy. We tensed in our beds in the darkness, expecting a sudden onslaught on ourselves and patients. We could hardly hope for survival now.

★ ★ ★

I suppose there had been black patches in my childhood in Kent, but in retrospect all seemed sweetness and light in contrast to the happenings in Hong Kong at Christmas 1941.

I was the youngest of eight children. Although we were not particularly well off with such a large family to feed, the thrifty way in which the household was run made it possible for us to live happily without any sense of deprivation. Most of our clothes were home-made, and expertly done too. Father had retired by the time I came along; he and Mother kept chickens, and garden produce was carefully tended. If we ever tried to refuse food put before us, we didn't get away with it.

"Picking and choosing bedad!" my Irish Mother would snort. "You should be grateful for what you're given. You'll come to your cuttings down one day, my girl!" This prophesy was used so often that it became part of family lore and I in time used it when my own children jibbed at clearing their plates.

By the time I was five I was an aunt, which gave me great status (in my eyes at least) over my schoolmates. Later, it fell to my lot to take my niece Kitty to and from her piano lessons. I yearned for piano lessons myself, but my parents had had my sisters taught without much success and had gone off the idea. I made such a fuss about having to escort Kitty and sit outside listening to her efforts that at last Kitty's mother offered to pay for lessons for me too. Alas, Kitty and her family soon moved to another county and my lessons came to a full stop, but I now had a basis and continued practising on my own — those few lessons have resulted in giving me many happy hours on the piano ever since.

From my earliest childhood, summer days seemed related to lavender. In our garden grew a bush which must have been planted long before I was born, as I always remember it as an enormous bush with gnarled and woody stems; when in full flower it completely covered a whole corner.

One sunny day, my Mother would decide that the time had come to cull the lavender. She would spread a large sheet on the lawn and proceed to cut the swathes.

None of us younger children was allowed to help with the cutting, but we were permitted to collect the bunches from her and lay them in rows on the sheet to dry out. The drying process took several days, after which Mother and we children would fill little muslin bags with the harvest, ready for distribution to friends, and of course for our own family use.

We moved house when I was eleven and my Mother insisted that the lavender bush went with us. Despite protests from my Father — upon whom the task of digging up the unwieldy bush fell — that it would not survive, the bush took no harm from its uprooting and continued to flourish, so the yearly ritual was still carried out. In later years when my older sisters had left home and travelled far and wide, their annual quota of lavender still went to them as far afield as India and Mauritius. ("Plenty stink!" grinned the Chinese postman when he handed me my lavender parcel in Hong Kong in 1927.)

There was not a lot of spare money for toys, but the few that came our way were carefully treasured. I once had a wax-faced doll whose features had to be veiled if she was taken out in the sun in case she should melt. Whether the sun was ever hot enough to melt her I don't know, but we certainly took no chances! A double-jointed doll was prized above all others; though not exactly beautiful, with knobbly knees and elbow joints, the china face — with eyes that could close — and flaxen hair seemed to our uncritical eyes sheer perfection.

Most of the time, however, we made do with families of four-inch high dolls costing a halfpenny each; they had cloth bodies stuffed with sawdust, china heads with black painted "hair", and china arms and legs from elbow to knee. On sunny afternoons during school holidays, a group of us would decide to "do dolls' clothes" in a favourite spot under a big tree, each bringing her box of dolls and dolls' clothes. I don't remember anyone aspiring to anything grander than a cardboard boot box as a container.

Seating ourselves in a circle, we would unpack our treasures and display the various cuttings of material we had gleaned from family and friends. It was the custom to have large families of these dolls, all named, and propped up against the cardboard boxes beside us. We did a lot of "changeys" (not knowing the word "swop") before the dressmaking started All the dresses were fashioned in the same style — a straight piece of cloth was sewn at the back, with a drawstring at the neck and two holes cut to accommodate the arms. Some had a plain hem, others might sport a frill of lace round the bottom. Petticoats were made the same way, but here a bit of lace round the hem was a "must". How our tongues wagged! We all became "Mrs" for these sessions, and the illnesses and doings of our various "children" provided the topics for conversation.

One of our companions in the sewing circle, named Elsie, made a great hit when she brought out for "changeys" several pieces of sprigged pink and white muslin left over from a new summer frock her mother had just made her. We saw Elsie wearing the dress next

Sunday (this being the era of wearing "best" on Sundays), and admired and envied her in it. The following Sunday when she was wearing the dress again, from a passing tramcar a lighted match was thrown from the upper deck; it fell on to the muslin, continued burning, and in a few moments Elsie was a pillar of fire. A passerby grabbed her bodily, climbed over a fence to some grass and rolled her in his coat trying to smother the flames, but Elsie died of shock. This was our first experience of tragedy. We put away our pieces of sprigged muslin, and in the course of time our young minds were full of other things.

★ ★ ★

Modern traffic and other conditions have robbed today's children of many of the joyous seasonal fun we enjoyed: skipping, hopscotch and spinning tops; the hoop season, when a variation to bowling your hoop along with a stick was the game of standing in a row and twirling the hoop round the body, counting the number of times we could keep it up. (The much later craze of "hula hoop" was just a case of history repeating itself.)

★ ★ ★

How unworldly we children were then! When we reached our new home in Gillingham, I suddenly realised that the family cat had not accompanied us, announcing "We've forgotten to bring Tiddles!"

7

"We'll go back for her in a day or two," said my Mother, "She will be all right."

"I'll go and get her now," I decided.

"You'll do no such thing! Tiddles can look after herself, and Mrs. Gent will feed her if she's hungry."

I just couldn't understand such a callous attitude; surely Tiddles would wonder where we had all gone? When Mother was otherwise occupied I slipped out of the house with my ricketty old doll's pram and pushed it the two miles back to our old home. I soon found Tiddles in a box in an outdoor shed; she didn't seem at all pleased when I picked her up and cuddled her before putting her in the pram. It was a bumpy ride; Tiddles swore a lot and looked most unhappy.

Though acting against orders, I felt sure the family would be delighted at what I had done as soon as I produced Tiddles, but I was wrong.

"Now why did you have to do that?" my Mother demanded. "I told you she was quite happy where she was; I wanted to leave her to have her kittens in peace."

No one had told me Tiddles was expecting kittens, and I knew nothing about the anatomy of cats to make me suspect.

★　★　★

How much I envied my sisters when they were in their teens! Living in a naval town with plenty of male escorts, they always seemed to be going to balls and dances, and I shared the excitement as they helped each other into their exquisite dresses. They used to save their little white programme pencils with tassles for me.

They all worked hard too; my niece Kitty's father died when she was small, and her mother, my eldest sister, then trained as a midwife; one sister became a professional dressmaker, and another one started off as a pupil teacher at my school (her first task on entering my classroom was always to send me out of the room for talking), then went on to Spain as a governess. Most of them married quite young.

★　★　★

As was quite usual in that era, I left school at 13, and got a job in a bookshop and printers, which suited me down to the ground as I was always interested in books. I enjoyed being called "Miss Wells", and put my hair up. When plasticine was first put on sale, I was allowed to experiment with it, and a sample of my efforts was put in the shop window as an advertisement, to my great satisfaction.

Once, we had in stock a certain book which, from reading book reviews, I knew was considered very daring. When I got the chance, I pushed the book firmly to the back of our highest shelf, and felt quite justified in declaring to a would-be customer that we didn't have that book in the shop. Another time, I don't know what got into me but I inked my initials across the width of a book. Of course I was found out by my incredulous senior, and the book was taken to the guillotine to have enough shaved off to eliminate the offending initials.

I grew up at the shop, graduating to boyfriends, although parental control meant that I could only be "walked home" from work, and to and from church, until I was about seventeen. Such spare time as I had was spent in church-going on Sundays (Mass in the morning and Benediction in the evening), cycling and skating. It was on a skating rink that I met my husband Will who worked in the Naval Dockyard as an electrical engineer. He was one of a long line of boyfriends, but before long he was the only one and we became engaged just before the 1914 War broke out, intending to get married as soon as the war was over.

Will, an enthusiastic motorcyclist, was anxious to join up as a despatch rider. I think the fact that the new Triumph machines were being issued to applicants who were accepted helped to inflame his patriotism. To his bitter disappointment, the Dockyard refused to release him. Before long he was transferred to Invergordon in Scotland where a small repair dockyard had been established. Here he was earning extra money through overtime, and found life in Scotland rather lonely so wrote me that, as we could now afford it, we should get married right away.

So I resigned from my job and prepared for my wedding, and my first real journey: although twenty years old, I had not travelled further than short railway journeys to relations. One of my sisters accompanied me to Euston where I was to meet the wife of one of Will's colleagues who was to travel to Scotland by the same train. My sister had to leave me on my own in order to catch her connection back to Kent, and I felt very scared, sitting anonymously in London and about to be married the next day with no family to support me. The said wife and I were not known to each other, but I had been told to look out for a young woman carrying a small baby. I had already begun to wonder what I would do if by any chance she did not materialise, but she did and soon we were on the night express. Several young soldiers came into our compartment and immediately settled themselves down to sleep. I tried to sleep too, but the general excitement and the noise of the wheels kept me in a state of drowsy restlessness until the very early hours.

When I awoke the train had stopped. Snow was thick everywhere. Some of the soldiers were getting out on to the platform. Trolleys with cups of tea were being pushed along beside the train.

"Would you like me to bring you a cup?"asked one of the soldiers. "They won't serve civvies."

Gladly we women accepted the offer, and watched him come slithering back with two large mugs. The tea was lukewarm but we were most grateful to have had it delivered, for we could never have walked across that slippery platform ourselves.

Soon the train moved on into a world of whiteness. Never had I seen such snow as this. I was thrilled to see herds of deer ranging the hills. Someone said that the snow ploughs had been brought into use on the engine, and now we noticed the gradual slackening in speed as the gradient increased.

The train reached Inverness two hours late — long past the hour arranged for Will and I to appear before the Registrar at Inverness Castle where certain formalities had to be gone through as I had not had the three weeks' required residence in the area. We hurried to the hotel where we were booked, and freshened up, trudged up to the castle and completed the formalities, then were free to go to the church. I didn't dare say I was almost starving and far more interested in a good meal than getting married at that moment! When we reached the Catholic church, it transpired that the priest had had to go off to an emergency sick call and his time of return uncertain. We decided to return to the hotel for a meal, then tramped back to the church to be married. This wedding day of ours could hardly be said to be traditional, when I remembered the weddings of my sisters which were big family affairs, with everyone dressed to kill!

★   ★   ★

We began our married life in lodgings near Invergordon. To me, everything in Scotland was a novelty: for instance: there was our landlady's pig. Many folk in this area kept a pig, feeding it on household scraps and fattening it up for sale locally. Not having a sty, our landlady boarded her pig out with a neighbour who did have one, and I was taken on a state visit to see the pig and invited to scratch its back. When the animal reached the required weight it was sold at sixpence halfpenny per pound. The landlady bought another piglet which escaped from its sty and disappeared. I joined in the hunt for it, following the main road which led past a large church at the top of a flight of steps. A sentry of the Camerons Regiment was on guard at the foot of the steps as the road led to their camp.

"Hae ye seen a wee pig?" the landlady asked him.

"A pig, did ye say?"

"Aye, just a wee yin, about so," — she indicated the size with her hands.

"I did see a wee white doggie on the kirk steps, " he said, "but I dinna ken where it went."

We ran up the steps. The porch door was ajar, and out came the piglet. He had been to church. Seeing us, he turned and went inside again but the landlady chased after him and amid excruciating squeals, eventually cornered him.

★　★　★

After a few months up north I began to feel a bit homesick. Like the other men in the Dockyard, my husband was having to work long hours and the loneliness got me down. These were not the days when a housewife with time on her hands automatically went out and got herself a job. I did not like to let Will know how much I was missing my family and friends, but he must have guessed because, when a letter arrived from Kent telling me that my only brother (now in the Royal Flying Corps) was soon due for a short leave from France, he suggested I make a visit to England to see him. I jumped at the chance, especially delighted when Will was able to arrange for me to travel south with one of his colleagues.

Off I went, Will returning to bachelor quarters on a ship in the bay which was being used as a barracks for dockyard personnel. While down south I decided to buy a puppy thinking it would be company for me back in Invergordon. When Will met my train back, he said he had not been able to re-book our original lodgings, but had found other accommodation out of town. Carrying the puppy, I was taken to the new abode which was about two miles from Invergordon, along the road which skirts the shore of Cromarty Firth.

My heart sank when I first saw the place: two white-washed cottages of the "butt and ben" type stood by the roadside, looking lonely and desolate. The taxi driver helped us dump the luggage in a covered passage between the two cottages, and Will and I went through a wooden gate. My, what a transformation scene! A garden ablaze with flowers and full of shady fruit trees met our eyes. A well complete with buckets and pump lent an air of romanticism, though after a few days of having to collect water from it, "romantic" was the last adjective I would apply to it.

Before we reached the back door, our new landlady, old and stooped, came out to greet us. This she did by pointing to the dog in my arms and saying "Ye canna bring yon dog here."

"But it's only a puppy —"

"It canna stay here," she repeated. "My cat will na' abide a dog."

14

Will pointed out that we couldn't dispose of the dog there and then: we must keep it overnight and would arrange something about it the next day; we took the puppy up to the little attic bedroom we were to occupy and firmly shut the door.

The old lady — Mrs Husack — had prepared a nice meal for us in our downstairs living room and seemed a little more affable, although she still looked like a witch to me — even more so when the said cat (a huge black tom) arrived home.

That night Will and I discussed just what to do with the dog. He couldn't take it away when he went to work in the morning as the landlady expected, as he would be travelling on the back of a friend's motorbike. It was obvious we could not keep him in the bedroom all the time, so the only solution we could think of was for me to stand outside the house with the puppy until some likely person came along whom I could ask to take him. So after Will had left, I covered the puppy with a cloth in a feeble attempt to keep him out of sight of the massive cat which I felt sure would make mincemeat of him if given the chance, and took him outside. I felt very desolate standing there in strange surroundings, about to part with the little dog which I had hoped would ease my loneliness. For half an hour not a soul came by. Then an old woman approached, leading a cow. Being scared of cows, I got back inside the passage between the two cottages and waited. Time passed but cow and cowherd did not, so I peeped cautiously out and found that the woman was seated on the grass nearby while the cow had a feed. Also, to my delight, I saw three young soldiers coming in my direction. Boldly, I stopped them and explained my problem and asked them if they would like to have the puppy. They promptly said they would, adding that there were several dogs at the camp and one more would not matter; they added that I could come to the camp and see him when I was passing. I did in fact see him many times afterwards, and he looked well fed and happy.

★ ★ ★

Mrs Husack improved on acquaintance and we became good friends, although I could never tolerate her cat. She taught me basic cookery and how to make lovely clear jelly with the soft fruits from the garden.

Washing day at the cottage was an eye-opener to me. All washing of course was done the hard way in those days before washing machines were dreamed of: but Mrs Husack's ways were even harder than my Mother's had been. On the first Monday I came downstairs with my washing and asked where I could find a washing board.

She fixed me with a stern look and said "We dinna fash wi' the like; they wear the claes oot."

So rubbing by hand was the order of the day. My rinsing was a bit sketchy as it was hard work getting water from the well. When I started to go into the garden to hang the clothes on the line, Mrs Husack pointed out "Ye have no' bleached them yet, they must go on the green."

I looked about but could see no large patch of grass in the garden.

"Come with me," she commanded and led me out along the road to the side of the house where there was plenty of grass on which she proceeded to spread each garment out flat. Then I was instructed to sally forth several times with a watering can to sprinkle the clothes with water.

I never did get the hang of working the pump at the well. Either I could not get the water to start flowing for ages, or having got it finally going, I could not stop it dripping when finished and had to call for help. Mrs Husack was amazingly patient about my shortcomings. She explained that dripping could not be allowed as if the well ran dry — which she cautioned could happen in very dry weather — then we would have to walk half a mile to the burn to fill buckets and carry water home.

★   ★   ★

I had my bicycle sent up from Kent and was then able to go daily into Invergordon, not only to shop but also to visit friends, for by now there were quite a number of people from the southern dockyards working up north. On one of my cycling jaunts I passed two riders on horseback, one an officer of the Camerons and the other a Naval man. I was puzzled at the sight of the latter; having been born and bred in a naval town, I was surprised to see a naval man on horseback; also, his face seemed familiar to me although I could not quite place him. When Will came home that evening he mentioned that HMS *Collingwood* had come into the harbour that morning and that the Duke of York was on board — then I realised I had passed the young man who was destined to be King George VI and father of our present Queen.

★ ★ ★

We left Mrs Husack's before winter set in because Will was warned that when the snows came our road would be difficult and often impassable, so we moved to new lodgings in a large house in Invergordon on the harbour front, opposite a jetty. Here the sailors daily disembarked from the ships in harbour for shore leave; also ships coming in from action in the North Sea sometimes landed their wounded at the jetty for transfer to the local naval hospital.

One morning I watched an almost continuous stream of men, women and children pouring on to the jetty from whence they were transferred to launches which took them out to one of the three warships in the harbour, HMS *Natal*. It seemed that a party was being held on the *Natal*, and our landlady was able to identify many of the local dignitaries among those arriving at the jetty

That afternoon I was shopping in the town with friends when there was a somewhat muffled bang from the direction of the Firth. We rushed along to the beginning of the shore road and saw a dense pall of smoke from where the warships had lain at anchor. Long before the smoke cleared, news came that something had happened on the *Natal*. We all stayed watching until dusk, by which time the outlines of two ships could be seen but not the third.

We heard no official report, but rumours from locals and people helping with salvage work spoke of a picture show which was to have been given on the *Natal* that afternoon; it was thought that the film equipment might have somehow caused the explosion. In daylight, a large part of the stern showed above the water, and it remained there long after I left Invergordon.

Such of the victims whose bodies were recovered were given a funeral with full naval honours. With practically the whole civilian population of Invergordon, I followed the long cortège to the cemetery beyond the town. Lord Jellicoe (of Jutland fame), Admiral Beatty and Admiral Sir James Madden were among those who walked behind the gun carriages.

Whenever I see seagulls now, I remember that lonely hulk in the Firth with a line of seagulls outlining its length.

★ ★ ★

Will's transfer to Rosyth Dockyard meant yet another move for us, and we took furnished rooms in a large house in Edinburgh. My sister-in-law and her family also had rooms in this house, and a girlhood friend of mine lived not far away. The menfolk travelled back and forth to Rosyth by train every day.

One evening when my friend and I went to the station to meet our husbands, we found the entrance barred and were told there would be no more trains that night.

"Ye had better get awa' home," added the porter. "There's talk of a zeppelin raid."

We had heard that zeppelins were trying to raid the east of England, and having to turn back because of very heavy rain, but we couldn't believe they would get as far as Edinburgh. They didn't this time, although because of the alarm our husbands had had to spend the night in the train in a tunnel outside Edinburgh.

About a fortnight later came the real thing. Most of the household had retired for the night, ourselves included, when we were awakened by a commotion outside and shouts of "Put out your lights!" There followed a deafening explosion. We leapt out of bed and peeped out of the windows and saw people running in all directions, it being about the time the audiences from theatres and picture-houses were coming out.

We could hear others in the house on the move, and Will suggested we get dressed and go down to the basement where the kitchen and landlady's apartments were. As we groped for clothes in the dark, there was a terrific bang nearby. Several of our windows shattered and we heard — and smelled — a cloud of soot come down our chimney. On our way downstairs we met the landlady roaming about with a candle. She said the other lodgers were already in the basement so we hurried on. The front door was wide open — evidently burst open by the blast. We kept hearing the horrible crunches of falling bombs as the zeppelins cruised around without let or hindrance.

At long last things quietened down and the visitors left. Next morning the whole house looked a shambles, with broken glass and soot everywhere. We learned that the bomb which had caused our house damage had fallen on a three-storey building nearby, having dropped through the attic skylight into the basement. The family living there miraculously escaped injury. Six large steps which had led up to their front door from street level were broken and tossed about. Five people died in a nearby doorway where they had gone to shelter. We heard that a distillery had been set on fire, but of no other non-domestic damage.

★ ★ ★

By the time our first child, Olive, was born in 1916, we were living in a ground floor flat in Inverkeithing, near Rosyth. Will's motorbike was his main hobby, although he seemed to me to get more enjoyment from the machine when it was dismantled on the kitchen floor than from driving the thing. Weekends became a nightmare, as then not only his machine, but also those of his friends, received his kind attentions.

As I complained, little did I realise that a new enemy was preparing to invade our home. Early one Monday morning some visitors called unexpectedly: I was not too pleased to see them, being in the middle of the week's washing, but as was customary in those days, showed them into our rarely used sitting-room. To my astonishment, all the chairs were marshalled in the centre of the room, with thin wires trailing all round them.

Neither the visitors nor I could account for this set-up; nor was I very much wiser that evening when Will came home and gave me the explanation that he was experimenting with something called "wireless". The wires were removed, but thereafter I was always coming across little pieces of equipment in the process of being assembled on to panels. Soon after, we moved into a little house in Rosyth itself, by which time the "panel" game had so accelerated that the wireless paraphernalia occupied half the spare bedroom, alongside the dismantled motorbike which had now had to be laid up because of war petrol restrictions. These were eased after the Armistice in November 1918 when the arrival of our second child was imminent. Will was delighted when he heard that from the 1st of December, private vehicles could be used within a 30-mile radius of one's home, so the day before — a Saturday — the kitchen was commandeered for the re-assembling of the machine, the weather being too wintry to do the job outside.

"I'm getting up early tomorrow morning to have a trial run," he said, setting the alarm clock.

He need not have bothered about the alarm — I woke him at 4 a.m. and his trial run took him into Inverkeithing to call the doctor and the midwife. Miraculously, the bike started without any trouble at all after its long period of inactivity. He knocked up the doctor then went for the midwife who, despite the wild wind and pelting sleet, climbed astride the pillion and rode back with him. A well-built Scotswoman in her late fifties, she used to say when telling of her trip afterwards, "I never thoct to see masel' on one o' they contraptions."

★ ★ ★

Now the bike was back in one piece again, I was pleased to see it stayed that way, living out in the garden under an awning. But the newer hobby, wireless, was gradually gaining ground. More and more apparatus and gadgets appeared, filling the spare bedroom to overflowing. Will's patient explanations of what wireless was all about fell on stony ground, I'm afraid, for I was fully occupied with the new baby, Barbara, and Olive, now a toddler. At this stage, Will was transferred to the Ordnance Depot at Crombie, seven miles from Rosyth, where we had a slightly larger house with plenty of garden.

"I'll soon build a shed out there for all my things," Will promised, but because so much of his spare time was taken up with wireless activities, the shed didn't get going until his father came to live with us. He was a retired carpenter, and since he had to share the spare bedroom with all Will's gear, it was in his own interests to build the shed as soon as possible, and this he did.

Now at last, I thought, we could have a reasonably tidy house, apart from the children's toys which could quickly be put away, but not coils of wire, boxes of screws, nuts and bolts, tools, and all manner of electrical gear decorating sideboard, dining-table and mantelpiece. We were also becoming inundated with regular deliveries of various weekly wireless magazines which were meticulously read, then stored for future reference.

★   ★   ★

With the shed finally in use, Will spent all his spare time there, fiddling with his wireless gadgets, and with his father off to the village club, I found myself alone evening after evening.

"Why not bring your knitting out to the shed while I work?" suggested Will when I ventured a complaint about loneliness, but sitting on a hard wooden chair among tools and shavings, beside an electric heater, when there was a cosy chair by the fire in the house was not my idea of a relaxing evening. In any case, there would not have been much room for me as Will was gradually gathering soul-mates with an interest in wireless and our shed became a regular meeting place for them.

One day Will told me excitedly that he had finished building a crystal set, which was duly installed on a table in the corner of the living room. Hour after hour he sat beside the set, headphones on, patiently trying to pick up signals in morse. From now on I had no reason to complain of lonely evenings! On the contrary, almost every night one or other of Will's pals turned up and sat round the table with him, taking turns with the headphones while Will manipulated the cat's whisker trying for sensitive spots on the crystal.

Every few days the set would be transferred to the shed for adjustments, and in due course Will began to pick up signals.

His experiments received an unexpected fillip when a young man called James was sent to Crombie by his company to service the huge accumulators in the generating station at the Depot where Will worked, for James proved to be as enthusiastic a wireless fan as Will himself. All James' spare time was spent at our house. Eventually his landlady complained to me as his hour of leaving us (or more accurately, "the set") grew later and later. Headphones clamped to their ears, the two of them sat over the set, jotting down signals with devotion and excitement.

Suddenly the pattern of action changed and they spent their evenings in the shed. At 10 o'clock I would make cocoa and sandwiches and call the enthusiasts in: they came, but continued their (to me) complicated discussions of coils, condensers and wavelengths. During this period the set on the table in the living room was not entirely neglected, but it transpired that something bigger and better was materialising in the shed.

One day they went shopping in Edinburgh. There was an air of secrecy about this expedition. When they returned, both looking jubilant, I could only see one small parcel which they unpacked with great reverence.

"Good heavens!" I exclaimed when all was revealed. "Another light bulb! Where can you use a silly little bulb like that?"

"That 'bulb' is a VALVE!" James explained triumphantly.

"And it's what will bring you music on the wireless later on," added Will.

"Later on: tell me the old, old story," was my caustic comment.

"Tell Mabel how much it cost," said James, "then perhaps she will show a little more respect for it."

Will hesitated, but I insisted. "Two guineas," he said.

I was furious as well as flabbergasted — two guineas was nearly a week's pay! It was patiently explained to me that this expensive item was for a new kind of wireless set which would give much better reception than the crystal set.

★　★　★

"I'll get you to buy me a frying pan next time you go to Dunfermline," Will said later that week. This demanded an explanation: he had made some coils for the new set and these had to be fried in paraffin wax. I was taken out to the shed to see the beautifully made coils, the intricate winding giving them the appearance of spiders' webs. Will's evident pleasure at my admiration of his handiwork made me realise I was being very mean in not showing more interest, and I decided there and then to remedy this state of affairs.

"Now I can get busy with those coils," said Will happily when I brought the new frying pan home — and how relieved I was to find he intended to deal with them himself. I had had an uncomfortable feeling that because of my newly shown interest, I might be delegated to do the frying. (Shades of hours spent in

26

the past rocking developing tanks during the home photography craze, and holding bits of fretwork in position when carpentry was on the go!) But I need not have worried: the frying turned out to be far too important a job to be entrusted to me.

The time came when the valve set was sufficiently advanced to be brought into the house for trials. A taller aerial than the one we already had was required: the new mast was delivered and it looked just the thing I had always wanted — a high pulley pole for the washing.

"If you fixed a pulley on it, you could have your aerial wire at the top," I suggested, but this didn't find favour with Will, although at least I did get the old aerial pole for my pulley.

Now the listening sessions in the living room began again, Will and James wedded to their headphones, ecstatic when they could pick up voices above the distortion and interference from atmospherics. Sometimes I was invited to don the earphones but, although I could catch voices occasionally, they were never clear enough to make out what was said.

When James, his allotted task completed, left Crombie, I more frequently took a turn at listening, which gradually became more interesting as reception improved. I heard P. P. Eckersley give a talk on how various notes responded to transmission by radio — he struck notes on a piano to illustrate, and while the tones of the middle octaves were true albeit somewhat tinny, the very top notes lost their tune completely and just sounded like wood being tapped.

★   ★   ★

Now that he was regularly picking up the testing stations, Will had to try for something more ambitious — the continental stations. He spent hours searching for a Dutch station at the stated times of relay, one such being a Sunday afternoon when rain had prevented me from taking the children out for a walk, and we three were indoors round the fire while Will sat intently listening at the table. The children, like me, understood that there must be perfect silence when Will was at the set, and picture books kept them quiet for a while. At length Barbara (now four) tired of sitting still and climbed on to the revolving piano stool and idly turned round and round on it. The stool developed a squeak which was already exasperating Will when even worse happened — the seat worked up so high that it fell completely off its base, Barbara with it. Feeling in disgrace over the commotion and yelling of the child, I rushed her upstairs to quieten her. I had hardly got up there when Will called for me to come at once. Thinking that Olive too must be offending in some way, I rushed down. Will's face was radiant, his rapt expression of one having a vision.

"I've got it!" he cried. "Come and listen! They're playing the Ballet Egyptienne!"

I put the headphones on, and sure enough, heard the faint strains of an orchestra playing this very piece which I was struggling to learn on the piano. Will's delight knew no bounds. Before long the whole village knew about it. Many of his buddies whose early enthusiasm had waned, now revived their interest, and the following Sunday afternoon some of them came along to take a turn with the headphones to hear a relay from The Hague. It was just as well I was no real enthusiast myself, as now my chances of "having a listen" were rather slim.

So the pioneering went on. More coils were wound, panels were altered; then the whole contraption would suddenly be dismantled and out of action for a few days before being restored to its recognisable form. Our whole home was now a wireless den. I found myself being urged to go to the village whist drives in the evenings so that Will and his cronies could pursue their discussions and experiments without let or hindrance. As hobbies go, we had come a long way from motorbikes in pieces on the kitchen floor!

★ ★ ★

An ardent band of listeners gathered round our set for the first programme from Marconi House in November 1922. Reception was quite good, though atmospherics were still a bugbear. Will assured me that all this would be corrected in due course; in the meantime he built a larger set with four valves.

His corner of the living room was a sight to see: the painstakingly assembled components comprising the set certainly produced the magic of audible programmes, but were fully exposed to the light of day. Not content with the table which held the set, Will was now also monopolising the adjacent window sill with batteries and gadgets, while my pot plants were shoved further and further along — or sometimes even dumped on the floor when he had run out of space. Goodness knows where the next encroachment would have been had his father not decided to build a cabinet to contain the set and all its paraphernalia. It was designed like a bureau with a front flap coming down flat as a table; the set was inside, and below a compartment, also with its drop-down flap, was to house the batteries. When not in use, the whole cabinet could be closed up to look like a piece of furniture.

The moment it had been put together, though unvarnished and unpolished, Will insisted on tranferring it from the shed into the house to see how it looked; needless to say, it had come to stay. Neither his father nor I would agree to the cabinet being sand-papered and painted in the house, and Will would not hear of it going back into the shed once the set was installed in it. This was the situation when Grandad received an invitation to visit his eldest son in America, and sailed away.

"I'll finish the cabinet off one of these days when I feel in the mood," Will promised.

Despite its naked appearance, the cabinet was certainly ideal from my point of view. At first the flaps were closed up daily as intended, concealing all, and my pot plants were once again in possession of the window sill. Then gradually, little oddments of equipment began to accumulate on the front flaps until the day came when it was too much trouble to move them off to close the flaps at night — so the flaps just stayed permanently open. The only saving grace was that all the clutter was concentrated in one place instead of being all over the room.

Grandad stayed in America for over a year. The day before his ship was due in Glasgow, Will's "mood" came on with a rush; he removed all the internals from the cabinet and hastily slapped on varnish. It looked dreadful and he knew it.

One of his father's first remarks when he entered the house was, "Oh, you finished the cabinet then."

"That's just camouflage," Will grinned. Later, his father took possession of the cabinet and worked on it in the shed until he made it what he called "fit to be seen".

The result was that all the villagers for whom Will had built sets now wanted cabinets, and Grandad found his services so much in demand that he had to build a workshop of his own in the garden.

★ ★ ★

Yet another home industry was embarked upon when Will set up his own battery charging service. Hitherto, local wireless owners had taken their batteries into Dunfermline — 1s 6d return on the bus and only a thrice-weekly service — and left for a few days before collection, incurring another 1s 6d return plus 1s charging fee. Many a load of batteries had also travelled back and forth in our latest means of transport — a motorbike and sidecar combination — often crowding me out so that I had to ride pillion instead of in the sidecar.

For some reason, the shed was not the place chosen for the charging operation; according to Will, the only place suitable was on the fitted wooden lid across the bath in the scullery. This meant that hot baths had to be snatched any night that no batteries happened to be on charge. Luckily, the children were still small enough to use the portable zinc bath in front of the living room fire.

★　★　★

The arrival of our first loudspeaker brought a fresh influx of visitors to experience this marvel of hearing programmes without taking turns at the headphones. The word went round the village, and Will was invited by the committee of a neighbouring village to give a wireless demonstration in its local hall. To many of the audience — mainly middle-aged and elderly — this was their first introduction to wireless in any form, and the wonderment on their faces was an entertainment in itself. Our mobile greengrocer lived in that village, and next time he came round with his horse and cart, I asked him how he had liked the broadcast.

"Well, noo, lassie, it was awfu' clever, ye ken," he said, "but there was just one thing missing — the body on the stage." I can hardly think he lived to see television with "the body on the stage" as he was pretty old at the time of this demonstration, but obviously he considered such a prospect completely beyond the realms of possibility.

Following on the success of this demonstration, we wrote to Glasgow Broadcasting Studio and asked if some dance music could be relayed on a certain evening. Glasgow readily co-operated and invited us to send a programme of what we would like to hear. Will borrowed three loudspeakers from a wireless shop in Dunfermline and set everything up in the village hall. The dance was a huge success: how rewarded the musicians in the studio would have felt could they have heard the vociferous applause from the dancers after a riotous eightsome reel!

Crombie was by no means dependent upon broadcast music for its dances — it boasted its own band! Despite being decidedly an amateur pianist, I was persuaded to take the place of the resident one when she left the village; even Will, who had never played a note of music in his life, was roped in to play the double bass! My musical career came to an end with the arrival of a third daughter, Mabel, in 1923, by which time the wireless was providing us with a goodly selection of home entertainment, such as dance music from the Savoy Orpheans, and humour from John Henry and Blossom, Mabel Constandurous and Oliver Wakefield.

One of the most important outside broadcasts was the opening of the Wembley Exhibition by the late George V. Our living room was packed to capacity that morning. As the exterior of the house was being painted at the time, the audience included the painter outside on his ladder with his head through the open window. Reception was perfect; the increasing sound of the approaching military bands, fading as they passed into the distance; the clarity of the orders given and the click of heels as companies sprang to attention, made us feel as though we were actually seeing it all.

No sooner had we got used to regular broadcasting from British and Continental stations than Will took up a new challenge. It was reported in one of the wireless magazines that some readers had picked up American stations, so when 2LO closed down for the night, the hunt was on — the quarry, America. Every night that atmospheric conditions allowed, Will and an equally keen friend sat down with their earphones and listened and twiddled knobs long after I had gone to bed. Success came after some weeks. One night I was summoned from sleep to come and listen. I could hear music, rather thin and crackly, but it WAS from America, and that seemed a miracle in itself.

After that, many a husband in the village braved his wife's displeasure and joined in the all-night sessions in our house. All this progress resulted in increased requests for Will to make more sets and for his father to make the cabinets, but our original set was still open as always as Will was still continually tinkering with its internals for improvements. I put in a request for a new all-embracing cabinet, and Will's father produced a real beauty on the lines of a roll-top desk standing on curved legs, with a concealed shelf beneath for batteries. Alas, we didn't enjoy it for very long — out of the blue Will heard he had been posted to Hong Kong for three years.

34

CHAPTER
TWO

Going to Hong Kong (twice)

At first I did not relish the thought of leaving Crombie where we had been so happy for seven years. The children knew no other home. There were safe roads and lanes for them to ride their bicycles. The village school was so near that Olive and Barbara could walk there and back unescorted. There was a rocky shore for swimming at Crombie Point if you felt like a two-mile walk, which we occasionally did in the summer. A recent amenity was the village tennis club, whose courts were just opposite our front door and, although most of us were amateurs, enthusiasm was boundless.

It seemed dreadful to be uprooted from what to us was a very full and contented life, but gradually the excitement of preparing "to go abroad" softened our regrets. Incredibly, in those days, the Admiralty used to tranship at its own expense all furniture and chattels of families sent for tours abroad, and ship them back again at the end of the tour. We had to decide which things to take to Hong Kong, which to sell and which to throw out, and kit ourselves in what we hoped were the right clothes for a semi-tropical climate.

In due course great packing cases were delivered to our back garden and covered with tarpaulins, in readiness for packing up. In the meantime, our girls and all the children in the neighbourhood played hide and seek among the corridors between the packing cases. Thank goodness the actual packing was done by the firm which was to arrange the shipping by cargo ship. Our beautiful new cabinet wireless set was sold as it stood, but Will personally packed a case of various items of wireless equipment to build another, and this treasure travelled as hand luggage with us and was not entrusted to the vagaries of a cargo ship.

★   ★   ★

Once over the first bout of seasickness, life seemed heaven on the P & O liner *Rawalpindi* (destined to go down valiantly fighting as an armed cruiser in World War II). Nothing in our former existence had prepared us for this life of lazy luxury. I especially appreciated sitting down to meals I hadn't shopped for and cooked. The children had the time of their lives, although this was before the days of nurseries or playrooms on board.

Going ashore at foreign ports was like stepping into new worlds. Of course we were duped at Port Said, not realising in time that we were being led by a friendly guide only to shops of his choosing for his commission. When I showed interest in several bolts of silk while trying to decide which colour to choose for a dress length, I found to my horror that an eager assistant had immediately cut a length of all three which I then had to buy. Moreover, after the ship left Port Said and I examined the materials, I found each length only measured one and a half yards, whereas my generous proportions required at least four and a half!

★ ★ ★

Although very excited on our arrival in Hong Kong, I found the first days most depressing. It was the height of summer. We were accommodated temporarily in a small boarding-house where the rooms were hot and airless, and the meals too rich and spicy for the children. There was nowhere for them to play other than in our two rooms, and I didn't dare let the two elder ones go off on their own (as they were used to doing in Scotland) beyond the confines of our lodgings. I had a dreadful attack of "Hong Kong dog" which is the worst kind of bilious attack you can imagine — I was convinced I was going to die. Poor little Mabel developed water blisters all over her body which caused great distress as they had to be pricked and creamed.

Barbara wrote a poem which summed up our first impressions of Hong Kong. It began:

Where the sun is hot and the earth is dry
And the babies wander around like a fly,
Is my dwelling place for quite a few years,
Though if I stay much longer, I shall be in tears.

37

It's the dirtiest place I've ever seen,
And there's no grass like a nice, bright green.
I'd rather go back to my home in the North
And have a sail on the River Forth.

Fortunately, after a few weeks we settled in a pleasant flat in Kowloon — on the mainland across the harbour from the island of Hong Kong — with our own furniture and belongings about us. To Will, this meant getting busy again with his box of treasures. He commandeered a small table at one end of the kitchen and got to work. Like all Europeans, we employed a Chinese amah to do the household chores, and Ah Ng was none too pleased at the invasion of her domain, though like me she had to learn to lump it.

In due course a new set materialised and, in a cabinet, arrived in our living room, where the familiar headphones tests began again, with a new-found colleague Alan. This time the aim was to "get Shanghai". Alan spoke Chinese, but did not happen to be with us when Will first picked up a broadcast in Chinese, so he called Ah Ng to come and translate for him. She was terrified at the thought of donning the headphones, protesting, "No, no, I no likee. Makee fire, I t'ink."

We continued to coax, and at last she fearfully put the phones on, obviously still expecting to go up in smoke, but she couldn't translate as the speaker was using the Mandarin dialect instead of the Cantonese she spoke. Like most amahs at that time, Ah Ng's slight knowledge of spoken English was of the "pidgin" kind, but she was ever eager to learn more. One day I found Barbara giving her English writing lessons. Although teacher and pupil soon tired of the lessons, they bore fruit, for Ah Ng told me when I came home from shopping one afternoon that during my absence a delivery of soft drinks had arrived and she had signed the "chit" for me. I assumed she had signed her name in Chinese, but when the account came in at the end of the month, I saw that one of the receipts had been carefully signed "cat" which was one of the words Barbara had taught her. There was a look of pride on her homely little face when I showed her the chit and asked if she had signed it.

"Yes, missie, I write all same Barbara talkee me."

That chit still survives.

★ ★ ★

Once we got used to the enervating heat, the huge cockroaches, and the fear of burglars, we began to enjoy life in Hong Kong. With no housework to do, my only duties were shopping and looking after the children, all of whom were happy in their new schools. Olive was able to continue with the violin lessons she had started in Scotland, and Barbara piano lessons. Olive progressed so well that she was chosen to take part in a small orchestra which was asked to play at Government House at a children's party.

Every weekend, a dockyard launch took us to one or other of the lovely beaches; there were also short launch trips to Stonecutters Island within the harbour twice a week after office hours. Will could already swim, and the girls and I soon learned in that lovely warm water.

Everything in Hong Kong was so colourful. The wonderful materials in the shops, and the costumes of many nationalities made even a walk into town vastly different from a walk along the High Street in England. We often came across Chinese funerals, which varied from the simplest where a coffin was carried suspended by rope between bamboo poles, with a couple of weeping mourners with a band of calico cloth round their heads and a handful of followers, to a traffic-stopping cortège with several bands, each playing its own choice of suitable music (within earshot of each other), with lorryloads of wreaths and whole families of mourners.

Particularly memorable was the funeral procession of a murdered Chinese millionaire, the head of a well-respected family and supporter of Hong Kong charities. Because some members of his family had to travel back from America to attend (by sea, of course — this was 1927), the funeral had been put off until their arrival; in the interim the body had to be kept packed in ice, and gangs of coolies had been employed in a continuous stream to carry blocks of ice up to the victim's mansion.

The route to the cemetery was just a solid mass of people. A huge framed picture of the deceased was carried on a floral plinth. The large group of mourners was screened from the public gaze by what looked like a large white tent without any roof, all supported on bamboo poles carried by coolies. All the bands were arrayed in colourful costumes. Man-size wreaths were carried by coolies. Friends of the family followed in cars at a snail's space. The whole procession took over an hour to pass us.

When we moved to a flat on Hong Kong island, from the end of the terrace we overlooked the courtyard of a large house occupied by a rich Chinese family. One day we noticed a lot of activity down there, with electricians busily putting up lines of fairy lamps. Through the excellent grapevine service among house servants, Ah Ng told us that one of the sons of the family was about to be married.

Before long, groups of visitors began to arrive. As each reached the entrance, a few musicians in the yard played several bars of music; some got a more lengthy tune of welcome than others — maybe according to their degree of importance.

Next followed a constant procession of coolies bearing what I took to be gifts for the future home. Most were borne on wooden plinths, highly decorated, and the musicians again played short obbligatos as each lot was carried in. There was so much to see that I was loathe to leave home for shopping and tennis in case I missed something exciting. Firecrackers were continually being let off throughout the day. The decorated bridal chair was carried out of the house and courtyard — "to go catchee bride", as Ah Ng explained to us.

Very reluctantly I had to go to a tennis commitment that afternoon; on my return, I passed a large crowd of spectators gathered at the foot of the ninety-six steps leading up to our terrace. Rumour had it that the bride would soon be arriving. With the children and a neighbour, I stayed to watch. We were the only Europeans in the crowd. A beautifully gowned young Chinese girl came over to us and in faultless English asked whether we would like to accompany her to the house to see the ceremony. While thrilled at the idea, we said we ought to go home first and change into more appropriate garb, but she said there wasn't time as the bridal possession would soon arrive.

"You will be most welcome as you are our neighbours," she added, seeming really anxious that we should go in with her, so we did. She introduced us to certain of the company and we exchanged bows. Everyone we met was wreathed in smiles; I could not make up my mind whether in pleasure or at our odd appearance, my neighbour and I in sweaty plain white low-waisted tennis dresses and the girls in play clothes, among the glamorous and exquisite brocade garments of the rest of the guests.

We were taken into a large room with heavy blackwood furniture, and walls hung with silken panels and large family photographs. Men were ranged on one side of the room and ladies on the other. The mother of the groom was pointed out to us; she was seated on an imposing blackwood chair and wore a black silk long skirt and mauve blouse; her small feet did not touch the ground.

Amahs were continuously serving every one tiny cups of China tea. Thank goodness the cups were tiny as I did not care for Chinese tea but dare not refuse for fear of offending these kind people. I soon found out that drinking it quickly was no advantage, for as soon as one's cup was empty, an amah darted over to fill it. Not only was the tea the problem: in each cup floated what our interpreter explained was a "happiness nut", about the size of a small prune, which had to be chewed for ages before it could be swallowed. My jaws ached, and the children were finding it hard to hide their distaste of both the tea and nuts.

A great burst of firecrackers heralded the arrival of the bride. The groom was already with us, attired in a long Chinese robe and a hat with a scarlet band. Without understanding the language I could tell he was getting plenty of "ribbing" from his friends! He had not so far seen his bride, for this was a wedding in the old Chinese style.

She was brought in sprawled on the back of an old amah. We could not see her face as her beautiful headdress had a veil of seed pearls to keep her face hidden. The amah stopped before the future mother-in-law. The bride descended and made obeisance to the old lady by kow-towing, then did likewise before a photograph of the deceased father-in-law to be and was led to the head of a large table where she was joined by the groom. Her veil was raised as she stood with downcast eyes. Lengthy speeches followed, toasts and a kind of mock meal in which food was offered but not eaten. One dish contained a cooked chicken which had its head and legs fixed on slivers of bamboo; when the dish was passed round, the head moved up and down. We spectators were served with quartered mandarin oranges.

The ceremony at the table ended, the bride was taken away by the amah and other attendants. It was getting late; I told our Chinese friend we ought to be leaving, but she was anxious that we should go with her to see the bride in her bedchamber, and led us through to a beautifully furnished apartment where, surprisingly, amid oriental splendour stood a very English-looking brass bed. The bride was seated on a chair as the amah removed the wonderful head-dress.

"She must be glad to be free of it, after wearing it for so long," I whispered to our Chinese friend.

"You should not say that," she whispered back. "Nobody here understands English so it does not matter, but such a remark would mean bad luck for the bride."

I apologised at once, but she laughed saying "I don't hold with all these old superstitions. Neither do I intend to be married in the Chinese style if I do marry."

She introduced us to the bride; we bowed and gave her our good wishes which were translated into Chinese. As we left, our friend explained that the real wedding banquet was to be held the next night, and invited us to come. Intrigued though we were with all we had seen, we graciously declined: not knowing the relationship of our friend to the family we felt uncertain of whether we would be really welcome.

We saw the bride on the verandah of the big house many times after, wearing her ritual bridal dress which Ah Ng told us she would wear for a month. After that time there was another spate of cracker firing and excitement to signify that the time had come for her to depart with her husband to their own home.

★　★　★

There was plenty of social life in Hong Kong, including dances held at the Seamen's Institute which were really for the benefit of the naval personnel of whom there were always many in port. Will was not very interested in dancing, but he never minded my going. It was at one of these naval dances that I had what Wilfred Pickles might call one of my most embarrassing experiences.

For my birthday, Barbara — then aged nine — had bought me a very special present — "The best I've ever bought you," she assured me — a pair of fancy garters. They were made of orange and mauve shirred silk, with a tiny rosette of mauve and a little spray of minute flowers. They were the kind the Chinese girls wore on their lovely slim legs above the knee and which showed as they walked in their cheongsams with slit side-seams. On me they would be wasted, as skirts were then worn just above the calf, but I had to show enthusiasm about them, and after they had been duly admired by the rest of the family, I returned them to their box saying that such things of beauty could only be worn on special occasions.

When the girls heard that I was going to a gala dance soon after my birthday, Barbara immediately pointed out that here was a special occasion for the new garters to be worn. When I was dressing for the dance, she hovered around with the garters in her hand, and the delight on her face when I pulled them on was a sight to see. My intention was to remove them when I reached the dance hall and replace them with my everyday garters, but the memory of that happy little face changed my mind, consoling myself with the knowledge that they would not show.

There was a large crowd at the dance. All the naval men were in white summer rig and eager for partners. My first dance was with a very young sailor who had only just arrived in Hong Kong; he enthused about all the wonderful things he had seen in the shops, and how he was deciding what to buy for his fiancee in England. I handed out advice not to buy until he had had a good look round, and was so engrossed in conversation that it was some time before I felt something flapping round my right ankle. With horror, I remembered the garish garters! I dared not look down but felt my face flushing, so saying I felt a little overcome by the heat, I asked him to take me to my seat. There I saw with relief and astonishment that the garter was not around my ankle. In the ladies' room, I found both garters still in their rightful places. Thoroughly mystified, I returned to my partner and we sat out the remainder of the dance. While watching the other dancers, the mystery was solved: I noticed that the wide bell bottoms of the sailors' trousers were occasionally swishing against the ankles of their partners. While everyone else was happily ignoring the flapping, I had been only too conscious of it — but then they didn't have flamboyant garters on their minds as I had!

★　★　★

Old-timers in the Colony often talked about "Paddy's Market", said to be a bargain hunter's paradise, where thieves sold their ill-gotten gains. "Cat Street" was another name for it. One day a friend and I set forth to find the place which was in the Chinese quarter of the town. We clutched our handbags tightly, having heard that bagsnatchers and pickpockets were particularly busy there. There were long rows of stalls on either side of the road, as well as shops, full of everything you could think of, from everyday kitchen utensils and jewellery to sewing machines and tools.

If you handled an object you fancied, immediately a smiling Chinese assistant would be at your elbow, offering to sell it to you at "velly cheap price". You promptly cut his price in half and bargaining went on for some time, usually ending in you getting the article in question for at least one third of the original asking price, the assistant insisting that he "lose money". Not on your life! What he lost on the transaction was just that much less than he had hoped to make.

My friend bought a mincer for $2 (about one shilling in those days). Once it was cleaned up it looked as good as new except that the control screw was slightly bent. I borrowed it one evening but before it could be returned it disappeared. We then lived in a ground floor flat so if the kitchen door was left open it was only the work of a moment for a passing thief to slip in and grab whatever was to hand. Off we went to Paddy's Market again to buy a replacement, and there, among the melee of kitchen utensils, was the stolen mincer. Being so bright and clean it stuck out like a sore thumb, and the bent control screw was corroborative evidence. The salesman asked $3 for it.

"But I bought it from you last moon for $2!" exploded my friend. "Then bad man steal it and sell it back to you."

The salesman ignored the last statement, but agreed on $2, and my neighbour bore her mincer away in triumph for the second time.

★　★　★

At this time — the late 1920s — very few shops imported readymade clothes, so you bought your material from the tempting Indian silk shops and took it to one of the many Chinese tailors who made it up very efficiently cheaply and quickly. These tailors were very clever at copying styles from pattern books. Their premises — usually on an upper tenement floor which you reached by negotiating a flight of narrow rickety stairs — were always a hive of industry. One customer had her tailor make her a dress with a wide sash with broad ends hanging down. She decided the ends of the sash would look smarter if embroidered in red with some Chinese characters. The dress turned out beautifully but she was rather put out because every Chinese who saw her wearing it seemed to be laughing at her. Her amah eventually told her why: the Chinese characters on the sash were a fine testimonial to the tailor's workmanship — he had embroidered his name.

★   ★   ★

Well-to-do Europeans usually employed a cookboy, wash amah and a "makee-learn" (ie without experience) plus, if necessary, a baby amah and a gardener. We were very content to have just one servant, Ah Ng: after all, I had managed all the children and housework on my own in Scotland for years.

One couple had a cookboy whom they considered an absolute paragon — until one hot evening they returned home earlier than planned after dining out with friends, and found the cookboy sitting in a lounge chair in front of the open fridge, his bare feet resting on the bottom shelf.

★   ★   ★

The heat was also the cause of an embarrassing experience of a friend of mine who lived in Kowloon. One evening she went to a bridge party on the Peak; although it was a warm night, she wore a light shawl over her thin dress for the breezy trip on the cross-harbour ferry. On arrival at the house on the Peak, she left her wrap on her hostess's bed. During the bridge session, she grew increasingly aware of the constriction of her new bra, so when she was "dummy", slipped away to the bedroom to shed it.

The bridge party over, she took the cable car down to the lower terminus, then a rickshaw to the ferry concourse. As she walked towards the ferry, she felt a tug at her fringed shawl and turned to find the rickshaw boy at her side; he was holding out her bra and asking "Belong you, missie?"

Evidently the bra had become entangled in the fringe of the shawl as it lay on the bed, and she had travelled all the way from the house on the Peak with it dangling down her back!

★   ★   ★

There was the most rigid water rationing in Hong Kong during 1928–29 when no rain fell for a whole year. Houses and flats where water was laid on had a daily supply only at stated hours. Large tanks were erected on the waterfront and filled with water brought from Shanghai by ship. Chinese tenement flats and huts with no indoor supplies depended on communal standpipes which were strictly controlled and only turned on at certain intervals.

This caused lengthy queues, and many people had to wait through several "on" sessions before they reached the tap. There was a code of honour, though: people placed their containers (usually kerosene tins) in the queue and went about their other business, returning periodically to see if the queue was moving.

The drought situation was so acute that when the fire brigade opened the hydrants to extinguish a fire in a cracker factory, masses of people from neighbouring tenements gathered round to take advantage of this out-of-hours supply, and the police had to be summoned to disperse the crowds before the firemen could fight the blaze.

The drought broke the day we left Hong Kong for England on RMS *Rajputana* — a year earlier than planned because Will became ill, although he quickly recovered in a temperate climate. He was posted to Sheerness, Kent, built himself a shed in the garden and was soon back in the wireless business.

By now the shops had plenty of commercially produced sets, but at (to us) prohibitive prices; in any case, Will preferred the thrill of creating his own set. Before long he had a little clientele as of old, mainly bringing their sets for adjustment or repair. Now programmes were broadcast almost continuously, and hearing so clearly the Cenotaph Service on Armistice Day, Royal Command performances, tennis and cricket commentaries, it was hard to believe that only seven years earlier even tinny music between oscillations on headphones had been greeted with wonder.

Now there was a hint of even greater marvels to come — pictures of events might be brought to us in the same way as the sounds. Although this seemed too fantastic to be taken seriously at first, Will believed in it and read up all he could on the subject and began to tinker with new pieces of equipment. Long hours were spent in the shed, and early in 1935 he told me he was all set to "try to get something on the screen". He moved his latest creation indoors — a large open-topped wooden box with a peephole in the centre, and internals inside. Television test programmes were being sent out at certain times; evening after evening Will tried to get results on his creation but without success; like all his earlier productions, it began to do a shuttle service between house and shed for adjustments until at last he declared he could see the faint shadow of movement on the screen. None of the rest of us could see anything, but after further adjustments, the time came when we could see flickers of movement resembling venetian slatted blinds slipping slowly and endlessly down the screen — just like today's TV sets when something goes wrong.

"Look," he told us, "One day we'll get real pictures there instead of just frames."

I'm afraid we didn't believe him, but soon after we did see the shadowy form of a girl dancing.

At that stage Will was transferred to the naval establishment, HMS *Ganges*, in Suffolk, so we moved yet again, and with added responsibilities at work, somehow his TV never did get re-assembled. He did, however, make an electric "grandmother" clock which hung on the living room wall and puzzled all first-time visitors with its jerking jump, every thirty seconds, and by its exposed vitals as inevitably work on the outer casing ceased the moment the thing was working.

We were living in Shotley just outside the gates of HMS *Ganges*; Olive and Barbara were working in offices in Ipswich, Mabel at the village school, and Will and I were thinking of putting a deposit on a house in a new estate being built nearby. One winter's morning after Will had gone to work and the girls to their buses, I got down on my knees to clean the hated flues of the ancient cooking range and consoling myself with the prospect of the all-electric house we hoped to have before long, when Will returned unexpectedly.

"You can leave that job," he said. "Start packing your bags, instead — we're going back to Hong Kong!"

The last thing he and I wanted was the upheaval of another appointment abroad. Mabel was the only real enthusiast at first — anything that got her off school for a few weeks sounded a good idea to her — but when passports and luggage labels arrived, Olive and Barbara warmed to the prospective move, and Will and I decided to regard the next three years as an interlude which would soon pass; our dream house would have to wait a little longer.

★ ★ ★

In January 1938 we sailed from Tilbury on the *Kaiser-I-Hind,* then one of the P & O's oldest liners which shook and creaked her way through the Channel that first night.

I had never wanted to return to Hong Kong, yet it was almost a thrill to sail again into that land-locked harbour with the green hills of the island rising steeply on one side, and the background of lofty mountains behind the flatter peninsula on the other. We were met on disembarkation by old friends, and before long found that this tour was much more to our liking than we had imagined.

Our flat was in a block of six which was enclosed in palm-shaded grounds adjoining the Naval Dockyard, and only a ten-minute walk from the city. Four large rooms in a row were flanked on either side by wide verandahs. The first room led to the kitchen and servants' quarters. Magnolia and banyan trees and a tennis court added to the attractive grounds.

Our furniture had a very rough passage from England. Many items were damaged beyond repair. The top of our beautiful radiogram was completely smashed in, although surprisingly the valves within were intact and the radio functioned as soon as it was plugged in.

Will's old wireless colleague lived nearby. Their friendship resumed where it had left off nine years earlier, although now they searched for overseas stations with more sophisticated equipment. Hong Kong had its own broadcasting station, ZBW, whose broadcasts consisted mainly of gramophone records.

It was a relief to me to hand over the housework, cooking and washing once more to servants. On this tour we employed two, a general amah and a young "makee-learn" to help as, now with five adults in the household, there was a lot of washing and ironing.

My only chore, the shopping, became a social occasion. Most mornings I walked or took a rickshaw to the modern stone market to choose fresh foods, and invariably met a friend there. The ensuing chat took far longer than the actual shopping — in fact the owner of our favourite stall used to draw up two high stools for us as soon as we hove in sight.

I had the time to linger in the seductive silk shops, make purchases and then go home and run up dresses with the day's bargains on my sewing machine. Both Olive and Barbara took secretarial jobs with the Hong Kong Government. Mabel reluctantly enrolled at a small commercial school to learn shorthand and typing — she would have preferred to train as a nurse, but was too young. Nevertheless, she endured the commercial class, sustained by milkshakes and ice-cream sodas with her fellow-pupils at the Dairy Farm milk bar during breaks.

★   ★   ★

With plenty of leisure for swimming, tennis, mahjong, tea parties, whist drives and bingo, the disturbing headlines from Europe seemed very remote. Our major concern was what would happen to us if the Japanese should ever have the audacity to attack the colony. The newly formed ARP department was recruiting men and women to train as Air Raid Wardens — mainly Chinese, as most European and Portuguese young men were already members of the longstanding Hong Kong Volunteer Force. VADs were recruited among women and trained to nurse casualties in the Military Hospital if war came; also formed was an Auxiliary Nursing Service to provide nurses for civilian casualties, which I joined.

★   ★   ★

The weekend that World War II broke out, Hong Kong was tense and alert, but as the days passed without the Japanese making any move to attack the colony, we all breathed again. I joined a Red Cross group where we made up operation sheets, surgeons' coats etc. The girls and I knitted submarine socks, jumpers and balaclavas to be sent to England. Regular air mails from England, only started a year before, ceased, and letters now took months to arrive by sea round the Cape, as even the weekly P & O sailings were no more. Our bathing trips were limited to the nearest bays because the further ones were part of the newly defined defence area.

By now our family included three pets: Scot, a black chow puppy, a mynah bird called Peter, and Paddy, a small monkey. Scot grew into a handsome dog, adoring Mabel, tolerating the rest of us, and very businesslike with delivery boys, whom he always escorted personally from the front door to the kitchen, his nose very close to their heels.

Olive one day enticed me into a pet shop to see a full-grown mynah bird that had taken her fancy. "It really talks, Mum," she declared. "Wouldn't it be lovely to have it at home, and teach it things?"

The bird certainly could talk — but only in Chinese.

"Missie can teach bird talkee English," beamed the assistant, but I didn't feel equal to giving a bird English lessons so we left the shop empty-handed, but the seed had been sown, and soon after when some baby mynahs appeared in the shop we bought one.

Peter was beautiful; when the sun shone on him, the iridescence of his black feathers showed rich purples and bronze, but for nearly three months our concerted efforts to get him to talk resulted only in an incessant squawking that nearly drove us mad. He lived in an enormous cage on the verandah. Sometimes in desperation I threw a cloth over his cage to keep him quiet. Came a day, when the rest of the family was out, when I heard a little voice from the verandah say "Hello Peter!" He was mimicking Mabel's voice! He learned to greet each of us with "Good morning" whenever we went near him, using each of our voices in turn — including the amah's. He summoned Scot the dog in Mabel's indulgent one; he copied the unmistakeable guffaws of a group of ladies who often came to the flat to play mahjong. When Will took to sleeping on the open verandah during the summer, Peter learned to imitate his first resounding yawn so perfectly that I could not tell the difference between them. Every time the telephone or door bell rang, he would call amah in my voice, repeating the call in a more impatient tone if she did not respond quickly (and he didn't allow her much time!). He imitated amah calling each of the girls in turn to get up in the morning. His greatest achievement was his whistled version of *The Lambeth Walk*, complete with the final "Oi"!

Paddy the monkey joined our household strictly against my better judgment. Olive had always hankered to keep a monkey, and often lured me into pet shops to view some "dear little monkeys", but I firmly resisted her pleas. One afternoon while I was at a friend's house having tea, Olive phoned me: she had been haunting the pet shops again and been persuaded to buy a very small baby monkey which looked far too young to be away from its mother.

I told her to take it back to the shop at once, but she explained this was impossible, as she had fastened the monkey's chain to the cord of the sunblind on the verandah; he had promptly shinned up to the top of the blind right out of reach. I hurried home to find the monkey had got its chain hopelessly entangled with the blind cord. When Will came home he borrowed a tall step-ladder and mounted it with wire cutters, but his approach sent the terrified animal into a menacing frenzy and, fearing he would bite, I persuaded Will to give up for a while. All night we could hear the pathetic mewing, but by morning we saw Paddy had managed to untangle his chain and could now move quite freely within the length of it. He was still frightened, and shot up as high as possible every time any of us went near him.

After everyone else had gone out, I sat quietly in a chair beneath his perch, a cut up banana on my lap. The bait worked: after half an hour he ventured down a little, then suddenly darted over to me, snatched a piece of banana and sped away to the top of the blind. He soon returned and snatched another piece, this time sitting on the window sill while he ate it, never taking his eyes off me. I moved the remaining pieces further back on to my lap; up he got on his back legs and peered at my lap, leapt on it, grabbed some banana and leapt over to the window sill. The next time he came, he stayed and ate the remains of the banana sitting on my knee; I dared to stroke him, and he gradually dropped off to sleep.

Within a few days he was quite at home with us and nothing more was said about taking him back to the shop. He loved to perch on my shoulder (his chain round my wrist), and to sit on my knee while I was knitting. He loved to hold the ball of wool and pay the wool out to me when I gave a tug; sometimes he would drop off to sleep, then when I tugged at the wool and wakened him, he would chatter his little teeth at me and start pulling the wool off the ball as fast as he could.

Will made a special box for Paddy, fixing it high up in the corner of the verandah, his chain long enough so that he could come down and run along the verandah, or climb into the shrubbery outside which he quickly learned to use as a convenience. I took him for a daily walk in the grounds, always on his chain, and he revelled in scrambles among the bushes.

It soon became all too apparent that he needed a daily wash. When I first produced a bowl of water, sponge and soap, he grabbed the bowl and upset it, seized the sponge and retreated with it to his box where he pulled it to pieces. Eventually though he accepted daily ablutions as his lot, screwing up his eyes tightly when his face was being washed — in fact it was only possible if his threshing limbs were first swathed in a towel.

We tried him out in the bath and he obviously liked the idea of running from end to end with the water just up to his middle. He was intrigued when we turned the tap on; when it was turned off, he hung on with one hand while he bent down so that he was looking up into the tap, then he felt up with his fingers. Olive turned the water on very gently, and he fell back into the bath with surprise.

One of the girls showed Paddy a soft puppet. At first he seemed frightened of it, but soon adopted it as his own and was seldom without it, taking it up to his sleeping box and cuddling up to it. Sometimes it fell out of the box during the night; and when Paddy awoke and discovered it had gone, he woke me up with his whimpering until I got out of bed and returned it to him. After many such disturbances, Will made a second sleeping box and fixed it to one of the trees well beyond our verandah, and we put Paddy there at night; now, if he dropped the puppet he would either have to get down himself to retrieve it, or settle without it. This worked well — certainly Paddy always had it in his arms every morning when I went to bring him indoors.

One night we were awakened by a thunderstorm followed by a veritable deluge of rain, and I wondered if I dare pluck up courage to go out into the garden to rescue poor Paddy.

Will maintained that the tree and box were sufficient shelter, adding that monkeys in the wilds did not have umbrellas. Before I could force myself to take action, there came a clanking on the verandah, and then via the open french windows of our bedroom appeared a drenched little monkey, carrying his chain which he had somehow wrenched from the tree.

Later, he found he could sometimes undo the chain where it was hooked to his collar, and would suddenly be discovered scuttling about the flat unfettered. For sheer enjoyment he would shin up to the top of one of the mosquito-net canopies and use it as a trampoline. A favourite trick was to leap on top of Peter's cage and rock it wildly, until Peter's unmistakeable emergency whistle and indignant "Paddy naughty boy" brought one of us to the rescue. He was very friendly with Scot, though, and when I took them both out for exercise, Paddy would spring on to Scot's back and ride him like a jockey.

Once Paddy helped himself to a supply of Beecham's pills from the bedside table drawer, this misdemeanour being discovered the following day when the empty pill box was found under the bed, along with a very sick monkey.

★   ★   ★

Although things were going from bad to worse in Europe, and we were worried about our relatives and friends there, life was treating our little family very well. We loved our flat and its surroundings, all three girls were earning good wages and happy in their work, and I had the animals to keep me company during the day. Despite the very obvious defence activities in Hong Kong — exercises, practice blackouts, nursing training among volunteers, barbed wire on some of the beaches etc. — I don't think many of us visualised that war could come to the Colony. It was therefore a bolt from the blue when one afternoon at the end of June 1940 (when Hitler was invading a tottering France), Will phoned from his office with instructions for the girls and me to start packing our clothes at once: all wives and families were to be evacuated from the colony as quickly as possible.

CHAPTER
THREE

Being Evacuees

The next Monday morning, the girls and I with some two thousand other Europeans were shepherded on to the grey *Empress of Japan* which had been reconditioned as a trooper to take us to Manila in the Philippine Islands. Most of the public rooms had been converted into dormitories and crammed with tight rows of camp beds. Our family, with four other females, were allotted cabin accommodation. The cabin in peacetime had been meant for three passengers; now, additional double-tiered bunks had been squeezed in, and two camp beds were stacked in the narrow passage to the porthole which had to be kept closed and covered to conform with blackout regulations, so the cabin was airless. When embarkation was complete, our menfolk were allowed on board to say goodbye. No one knew how long we would be away, or where we would stay when we reached Manila. As an auxiliary nurse I should have been allowed to stay in the Colony, but there was a delay in the arrival of government permission to exempt me from the evacuation order; in any case, Will would not hear of my staying behind, maintaining that our girls must go to a place of safety and it was my duty to go with them and look after them.

The only member of our family who was happy when the ship sailed was Mabel. She had lately acquired her first boyfriend, George, just young enough to be evacuated with his mother, so here was a heaven-sent opportunity for the two to spend all day together. Two destroyers escorted us for most of the 36-hour journey, which was so rough that the little ships often disappeared completely behind great waves. Almost every one was seasick. In the dormitories in the public rooms, little provision seemed to have been made for babies, who had to share their mothers' camp beds.

★　★　★

Meals were served in the magnificent dining saloon, now furnished with plain mess tables with forms for seats. We queued at the door, and as diners finished and came out, a corresponding number was allowed in to take their places. There was not the staff to clear the tables quickly, so you sat down at first before a plate of the previous diner's leavings — enough to send those with queasy stomachs reeling for the bathroom before they had had anything to eat.

What a relief it was when the ship reached Manila safely. A deluge of tropical rain drenched us and our hand luggage as we disembarked. American marines carried our cases and shepherded us to waiting lines of small army trucks with tarpaulin covers.

American reporters pounced and pestered.

"Give us a story, lady!"

"Is it true the Japanese are spitting on English people in Hong Kong?"

"Did some of the wives really have to be frogmarched on to your ship?"

We were too wet, weary and heartily fed up to deny or confirm the wild questions. The steamy atmosphere inside the trucks was almost unbearable. A sorry sodden lot we were as the trucks drove into a large American army camp called Fort Mackinley, some seven miles out of Manila.

The accommodation consisted of blocks of wooden two-storeyed buildings set on stilt-like foundations to avoid flooding in the rainy season — i.e. now! Friendly marines helped us out of the trucks and led us in groups to our billets. We were made so welcome and helped in every way that it became possible to begin to enjoy the novelty of our surroundings. The camp beds and bedding, complete with miniature mosquito nets, were all spanking new. The washhouse was a shock at first — rows of lavatories and shower bays open for all to see, but we soon recovered from our initial reserve and showered happily six or seven under each nozzle, giggling like schoolgirls.

The dining-hall was about one hundred yards away from our particular block. Outside there was a queue to receive first a tin mug, dish and cutlery, then generous helpings of delicious hot food from huge vats.

★   ★   ★

There was nothing to do at Fort Mackinley except queue for meals and mill about, seeking out friends in neighbouring blocks and reading news bulletins. There was no news of any trouble in Hong Kong, and we simply could not imagine why we had been removed from our peaceful life and pitchforked into a refugee-like existence. After a few days we were on the move again: two more shiploads of evacuees from Hong Kong were expected and our barracks were to be used as a clearing house for them, so we were allocated new billets in groups of about one hundred.

The girls and I were among a crowd sent to a Women's International Club in the heart of Manila. Once more (and again in pouring rain) we climbed into trucks and watched hopefully from under the tarpaulin for our new home. It turned out to be an old wooden building on two floors, empty except for a long table running the full length of the largest room. There was a verandah where all our heavy baggage was stored. Just as we arrived, coolies turned up with cartons containing new camp beds etc., and we got busy erecting them. With all the beds in position, there was just room for a gangway between the ends of the beds and the table, on either side of which were placed chairs, so there we were with dining room-cum-bedroom complete.

Our first meal was fantastic: a party of Filipino waiters from the swish Manila Hotel arrived and rapidly laid the table with snow-white tablecloths (the first we had seen since leaving Hong Kong), and full place settings for a banquet. An American Red Cross official called in and made a speech of welcome — that and the magnificent meal boosted morale sky-high.

After the table had been cleared, we decided to put up the mosquito nets. The Filipino houseboys produced some nails and hammered them into the picture rails at intervals; on to these we strung the lashings from our luggage and suspended the nets from the ropes. Because so many nets depended on such Heath Robinson arrangements, it was necessary to crawl into bed with the utmost care.

We were awakened next morning by the return of the hotel waiters who immediately laid the table for breakfast; then it became apparent that they were waiting to serve the meal so, unwashed, we had to wriggle into our clothes under our nets and beneath the sheets with an interested audience.

After breakfast there was nothing to do but tidy the beds and queue for a wash — there were only four bathrooms between 100 of us. The continuing torrential rain made it impossible to venture out of doors. Mothers with young children had dreadful problems: as well as trying to amuse and control the bored and puzzled children, they had to queue for a turn at the washbowls to wash out napkins etc. Makeshift lines for the washing were strung up on the verandah above our baggage, but the space was extremely limited and things took ages to dry in that damp air — this of course was not the disposable nappy era.

Dejected and bored, longing for letters from our relatives in Hong Kong, and apprehensive about what perils they might be facing there, just living for meals to break the monotony, we sat around on our camp beds. Despite the arrival of more evacuees from Hong Kong, most of us were still convinced that we would all be back home very soon.

After two days at the Club the rain let up a little. It was Sunday, and the girls and I ventured out to try to find a Catholic church, but the roads were still in such a flooded state that we had to give up and return to the Club. On the way we found ourselves outside the American Red Cross centre, so called in to see if there was any news of our future. There was nothing the kindly officials could tell us, but the journey was not in vain for we bumped into another little huddle of evacuees which included George and his mother who was a good friend of mine. They were there to plead with the Red Cross to find them fresh accommodation. They were part of a large group of women and children who had been billeted in the historic walled city of Intramuros. The so-called hotel where they were housed had evidently been used as a brothel. The beds were alive with bugs and cockroaches, and rats abounded. The tenements opposite were so close that leering faces peered through the evacuees' windows. To cap everything, they had been disturbed at night by would-be "customers" seeking admission.

The Red Cross arranged another billet with its customary efficiency, working indefatigably to ease our lot. With the great influx from Hong Kong they had not had time to check on every billet which they had to find at short notice, hence some were not up to standard.

Kindly officials were always popping into our Club to ask if they could help in any way. One day, a lady came to ask for six volunteers to take up accommodation on a sugar plantation sixty miles away. Fed up though we all were, no one seemed keen to move that far from the town; also, we felt it might be a case of out of the frying pan into the fire.

"Would six friends come forward quickly, please?" begged the woman. "Transport will be here soon."

A sugar plantation sounded interesting though primitive — but at would at least be a change. I cocked a questioning eye at my friend Mrs Penney and her daughter Bettine, and she nodded assent.

"We'll go," I said, "but what are the sanitary conditions like?" Here at California Street, the plumbing was always going wrong, and I feared it might be back to thunder boxes out in the wilds, where the plantation seemed to be.

"I think you'll find everything OK in that respect," she laughed, taking our names.

* * *

Within the hour, the six of us were borne off in a great Cadillac driven by a Filipino who spoke good English. Along miles of straight roads we sped, past paddy fields and tropical vegetation; through native villages with Spanish names; pass endless statues of the great liberator Rizal; and at last, through wrought-iron entrance gates to Calamba Sugar Estate.

Any apprehensions about our new billet vanished as we were driven to a large clubhouse set amid smooth green lawns shaded by giant trees. A charming American lady, the wife of the manager, welcomed us, ushered us into comfortable easy chairs, and sent for coffee and sandwiches. She explained that some of the American staff were on leave in the States, and their bungalows on the estate had been offered to the Red Cross for evacuees, some 25 of whom had arrived before us.

The luxury of the bungalow to which we six were allotted took our breath away. Set high on stilts and reached by a short flight of steps, it was fashioned entirely of nipa palm, which is rather like bamboo, notched at intervals and extremely tough. The walls were made of the palm leaves, split into narrow strips then woven into a basket pattern.

From a wide verandah, insect-proofed doors led to two identical rooms, each furnished as a bed-sitting room including desk, telephone, and two of the largest beds I have ever seen. Adjoining each room was an enormous bathroom with tiled sunken bath and every gadget invented for ablutions. When we saw the mother-of-pearl toilet seats, I recalled with some embarrassment the misgivings I had voiced about the sanitary arrangements!

What a joy it was to have a real cleansing, unhurried soak with unlimited hot water, after the hasty washes on the ship and subsequent billets. I think this was the first time we had felt really happy since leaving Hong

Kong; it was marvellous to hear the laughter of the four girls from their bedroom long after the lights were out.

More pleasures awaited us the next day. Our bungalow was about a mile from the clubhouse where all meals were served, and a car called to take us there. Everywhere was so beautiful; velvet lawns edged with exotic flowers, long avenues of fine trees whose branches met and intertwined overhead; stretches of sugar cane, trim hedges enclosing the neat little dwellings of the Filipino employees whose fat, laughing children played in the tiny gardens.

Breakfast — a meal fit for a queen — was served on the cool verandah of the clubhouse, where we met up with several old friends and exchanged experiences of our former billets. Every facility on this estate was open to us: the library and cinema; the recreation room with bowling alleys and billiards; and the swimming pool and tennis courts, both floodlit for evening use. The remaining few American employees treated us as honoured guests, not refugees. One day all thirty of us were driven in a fleet of cars to a distant coconut plantation with a quarter of a million trees. A freshly picked nut was deftly stripped and pierced for every one of us, and we drank the refreshing liquid. There was a conducted tour of the coconut factory to watch the nut fresh from the tree go through all its processes to produce oil for commercial use, coir fibre from the external husk, and the dessicated coconut we keep in our larders. I have much more respect for half a pound of coconut now I know how it got that way.

The girls and I went to Mass on Sunday in a very old church in a sleepy village a few miles from Calamba, and were astonished to find that all the statues and Holy Family pictures showed the subjects with dark faces; in our insular way, we had never considered that every Christian thinks of Christ as looking the same as himself.

★   ★   ★

A few letters from Hong Kong began to trickle through. There was still no mention of any trouble or threat to Hong Kong, but all the writers said we were to be sent on to Australia. Will wrote cheerfully and advised us to select Sydney if we were given any choice. It sounded depressingly definite, but we hoped and prayed for some political miracle to remove whatever threat hung over Hong Kong, and prevent our further banishment.

Despite the lovely surroundings and luxurious life, we grownups were restless with anxiety about the future. The younger children were dashing from one delightful pastime to another, wearing their mothers down and getting on everyone's taut nerves. In desperation someone suggested they did some school work every morning, and Barbara eagerly volunteered to take charge — she had always wanted to be a teacher, office work being very much a second choice.

On 23rd July, after we had been away for three weeks, a special broadcast from Hong Kong was arranged. Husbands drew lots and the lucky ones were allowed to give brief personal messages. That evening we gathered round the radio in the clubhouse, each hoping to hear a familiar voice. Although none of us at Calamba was fortunate enough to hear a relative's voice, several of those who broadcast were acquaintances, and even such a tenuous link with home was a comfort.

Next morning, after breakfast, the manager's wife took me aside and gave me the shattering news that Will had died suddenly the previous day. She had apparently noticed a brief report of this in the morning paper, and had immediately telephoned the British Consul in Manila for confirmation. A cable arrived later that morning; there was the bald announcement, and brief propositions for our future: we could proceed to Australia in due course with the evacuees; we could travel to England from Manila, or we could return to Hong Kong to pack up our home and then sail for England. We chose to return to Hong Kong, and sailed that afternoon, thanks to Mrs Penney who did all our packing, and to our hosts who arranged passages.

★ ★ ★

The girls and I discussed our future plans endlessly during the brief voyage back to Hong Kong. We agreed that we should aim to stay there until the war in Europe was over. The only misgiving I had was whether it was right to keep the family in the Colony in case trouble broke out there, but the girls had the optimism of youth and dismissed this anxiety.

The funeral had already taken place when we disembarked. Kind friends met us and looked after us. We learned that on the 23rd Will had felt ill at home. He wrote out a cable to me telling me to come back from Manila if I could, and sent the amah off in a taxi with it to the GPO. Then he telephoned the doctor, who came at once and was with him when he died suddenly as a result of a coronary.

The Admiralty had already organised our future: we were booked to sail for England in four weeks' time on the *Narkunda*. It took a week of argument to reverse this decision — the last thing we wanted was a long sea trip through submarine-infested waters to land in England during the Battle of Britain. We were eventually allowed to stay in Hong Kong because I was an ANS, Olive and Barbara were reinstated in their "essential" Government jobs, and Mabel fortunately had her 17th birthday during the negotiations so was now old enough to join the ANS. Once enrolled, she and I could be posted together if an emergency arose. She took the course but failed the exam. — for which I eventually had reason to be truly thankful. She got an office job with the Army so all three girls became the wage earners instead of Will.

Of course we had to vacate our lovely quarters in Naval Terrace, and moved into a flat in a tall white block curving round Gap Road in Happy Valley — within a stone's throw of Barbara's office and the race course and Jockey Club. Our front windows looked out on Morrison Hill, a barren rock which was being chipped and blasted away day after day. Our back view was over the Indian cemetery and Mosque. We were now living among a mainly Chinese community. From the bedrooms at the back, every tenant had a good view of the tenants of the other blocks. A party of dancing girls below provided almost non-stop Chinese music. The scent of their exotic powders and perfumes always hung on the stairway. Mahjong tiles clattered on hard tables well into the night; cheerful servants clattered pans (and tongues) in kitchens long after late evening meals.

I made friends with a neighbour, Connie, an Australian who was also an ANS. In response to a letter from a friend in Australia, we took her husband (a colleague of Will's) as a boarder. We were rather relieved to have a man in the flat where we were surrounded by so many strangers, few of whom spoke our language.

It soon proved impractical to keep Paddy in a small flat with no garden. After he escaped several times, leaping from one verandah to another and terrorising the neighbours, we had him put to sleep. Our dog Scot had died the previous year; his successor was a tawny female chow called Patsy. Peter did not seem his old happy self and gradually stopped talking. I found a growth under one of his wings and treated it as best I could but he died.

"Master want Peter," was the amah's consoling comment.

CHAPTER
FOUR

Invaded and Besieged

Hong Kong seemed so normal once the flurry of the evacuation had died down that it was no wonder the grass-widowers kept pressing the Government for the return of the evacuees, all now in Australia. Theoretically, all the British women left in Hong Kong were either in jobs which were considered essential in the event of an emergency, or else were members of a nursing or other defence unit. You might expect those who chose to stay behind with a view to serving in wartime to be considered somewhat heroic: not a bit of it! Their names were mud among the grass-widowers and the banished women. The trouble was there was no sign of an emergency, and while the evacuees were living in unfamiliar quarters on little money in Australia, the women remaining in Hong Kong were in great demand for office jobs and the social scene, enjoying all the luxuries the Colony could offer. It must be admitted that many women (including the girls and I) stayed in Hong Kong because it suited us — few really imagining that the Japanese would ever be so audacious as to attack us.

We found we could live comfortably on the three girls' combined wages. Most weekends we played tennis with friends or went swimming at Repulse Bay. There always seemed to be a boyfriend of one or other of the girls calling at the flat. George in Australia had been replaced in Mabel's affections by Sidney of the Royal Scots.

Nursing became my main interest. We of the ANS were invited to help at a small convalescent hospital where the patients were suffering from beri beri, mainly caused by malnutrition. I little thought as I watched the bloated bodies returning to normal that the time was fast approaching when I would be even more familiar with the manifestations of beri beri.

A cholera epidemic provided the ANS with more sobering nursing experience. We were given lectures on the nature of the disease and instructed in our duties. We had to wear shoes which could be left at the hospital each day and eventually discarded. Our uniform was to be laundered at the hospital, not brought home. The main isolation hospital building was used for patients who had recovered from cholera and were convalescing before discharge. We each did a week's duty in these convalescent wards before being sent to the nearby huts where the new cases were first received. These huts were single-storey brick buildings with concrete floors. Doors and windows were fly-proofed with fine gauze mesh, and at each doorway lay a heavy coir mat soaked in strong disinfectant to cleanse one's shoes before leaving the hut.

The first sight of the patients in the huts was unforgettable. The majority were of the coolie and labouring classes, and all looked as though their lives were draining from them. Their eyes were sunken and in many cases the skin was almost black.

On admission, each new patient was given an intravenous injection of saline. So dehydrated were some of them that it was difficult to find a suitable vein to take the needle. Thereafter, saline was administered by drip feed. The saline container was hung on a bamboo frame and had to be kept topped up until the prescribed amount had been absorbed. We were kept very busy with this, but those patients who had progressed beyond the drip feed stage were very helpful and would give warning when a neighbour's container was getting low, for they realised the necessity of the continuous flow. It was amazing to watch how soon the saline took effect; it seemed that if a patient rallied by the third or fourth day he stood a good chance of recovery, but many were too far gone on admission and died. Surprisingly, there were very few children among our patients.

Once the saline had improved their condition, they became aware of the terrific thirst which accompanies the disease, and were given as much kaolin as they liked to drink, and eventually tea and barley water. As they improved, some of them began to get artful and tried all sorts of ruses to avoid taking their pills and medicine. A certain pill which had to be given daily was greatly disliked, and it was necessary to put it right into each patient's mouth to ensure that it was taken. But even this precaution was not enough: some patients kept their pills in their mouths until we moved further down the hut, then spat them into the chamber pots under the beds. As the pills were mainly permanganate of potash, the purple traces were easily seen and the trick discovered, so it became essential to stand over the chief culprits until they had actually swallowed their pills.

One old man had a great objection to having his temperature taken. He would hop out of bed when he saw a nurse approaching and go to visit another patient nearby, then on to another, hoping nurse might forget about him. Another ruse was airily to wave away whoever approached with the thermometer. One day he thought up a new idea; at temperature-taking time, he was found enthroned on his chamber-pot, wrapped in a grey blanket and grinning wickedly.

"I'll just wait here till you've finished," said the nurse firmly. She had only recently arrived in the Colony as a new bride, and looking over the patient's wizened head at me, added "I came East for glamour and romance — now look what I have!"

Few of the patients could speak English, so we ANS had to rely on the Chinese nurses and ward boys to interpret for us when they had time. (We had a European nursing sister in charge, some trained Chinese nurses and ward boys — we were really only "makee learns"; the ward boys did all the menial jobs.)

One very ill patient tried so hard to convey some urgent message to me every time I attended to him that at last I collared a ward boy and got him to interpret. It transpired that this patient was a baker's assistant and belonged to a bakers' union. He wanted us to make sure that, if he died, his death would be reported to the union as he had paid in for his coffin and funeral expenses. At his dictation, the ward boy wrote out the patient's membership number and full name, and we assured him that his request would be made known to the hospital authorities. From then on the poor man became more tranquil and died soon after. I passed his paper to the right quarters, but doubt if his wish was granted, as cholera corpses had to be disposed of without delay — there was always a supply of coffin parts in the nearby outbuildings waiting to be assembled.

It was very encouraging to see how quickly those who survived the first severe stage of the disease soon cheered up. Faces which for days had been haggard and expressionless began to be wreathed with smiles of gratitude at our approach.

On my third week I was transferred to the female patients' hut. Among these women was one of the sweetest old ladies I have ever met. She was listed as a street sleeper. Eventually she was passed fit to be transferred to the convalescent building, but when told this she protested violently. Whenever I passed her bed she took my hand and chattered to me urgently and excitedly in Chinese. Via a ward boy, I found she wanted me to ask the doctor to let her stay where she was as she was "so comfortable". Poor old soul, to feel comfortable in what I would describe as the most cheerless surroundings imaginable! But to her whose usual bed had been the cold pavement, a real bed, shelter from the weather and regular meals represented untold luxury and comfort. I tried to have it explained to her that she would be even more comfortable in the convalescent ward, but she looked unconvinced: she knew that however comfortable it might be in the new ward, it would be one step nearer to her return to her pavement home.

Another female patient was very different from the others. She was a strapping young woman, working as an amah in the house of a wealthy businessman, and spoke English. She responded well to treatment, and as soon as she became conscious of her surroundings, strongly voiced her disapproval. She asked me to telephone her master as she could not stay in this place. She would not take my word for it that even her master could not have her removed until the illness had left her, and the Sister had to deal with her. Of course she had to remain and quietened down in due course, although she never relaxed her superior attitude towards the other patients.

Gradually the epidemic died down. It was a real joy to look round the huts and count the empty beds. When one reads of cholera epidemics of earlier times and considers the difficulties that faced doctors and nurses, one wonders how any of them survived, either patients or medical staff.

The neighbouring building was a leper hospital. We often saw the lepers walking in the grounds, the only sign of their affliction being the somewhat leonine look on their faces. I heard that the type of leprosy found in

Hong Kong was usually curable if taken in its early stages.

★ ★ ★

Later, we ANS were called upon to help out at various little clinics dotted about among outlying villages. One such was up in the hills — luckily my fellow ANS had a car which took us most of the way, but we still had a trying climb before reaching the little shack which had been erected for the clinic. Our patients were generally farmers or workers on nearby building sites. We were only equipped to deal with very minor ailments; anything more serious we had to report to our superiors. This was absorbing and interesting work, but I had to give it up after a while; I then weighed 15 stone, and the climb up the hillside proved more than I could manage — in fact, I felt when I got to the shack that I needed first aid as much as any of the patients!

I missed the interest of the nursing episodes, and the weekdays were very lonely, with the girls at work, and only Patsy the dog to keep me company. I took a job as a daily nanny to a young English baby Jean, whose mother had recently died. My work was pleasant and entirely supervisory, as a baby amah was employed as well, and for the first time since Will's death I began to feel settled.

We had by now got used to living with a potential emergency. Many people still maintained there would never be an attack on Hong Kong, even if Japan came to blows with the United States. Certainly to me (and many others) a local war never seemed so inevitable as to warrant the upheaval of going to Australia to join the evacuees. Yet by October 1941 the signs were plain for all to see, as witness extracts from Barbara's diary:

"November 12th — Churchill says if the Japanese and U.S. come to grips, Britain will follow U.S. within the hour. I'm a bit afraid Christmas won't come.

"November 13th — The rumour is that the Japanese are coming here this Saturday — Mabel heard it, so did Mr Hall (our paying guest).

"November 15th — Papers say Japan is calling up her reserves."

November 16th refers to Barbara's boyfriend, Arthur of the Royal Scots Band then encamped at Fanling in the New Territories: "The band came in to play in two Canadian battalions which have just arrived".

"November 17th — Once again, the Japanese look like business, and they can't call it off every time."

On the 29th November, she confided to her diary that she had bought an expensive box of her favourite chocolates "as a treat to myself lest it is the last of treats".

★　★　★

Next day there was a large-scale civil defence exercise and blackout. Our part in the ANS was to make for our appointed wartime posts at a pre-arranged time to test how quickly we could convert it into a relief hospital. My post was in the Jockey Club building in Happy Valley — a few minutes' walk from our flat. I accordingly reported there and helped set up beds and equipment in readiness for the patients we would expect in a real emergency to arrive from the Tung Wah Chinese Hospital in order to free that hospital to receive war casualties. We were astounded to find that this exercise included the transfer of actual patients from the Tung Wah; of course it was good practice for the organisers of the scheme and for us nurses, but surely caused much unnecessary discomfort to the patients, who were carted back to the Tung Wah in the early evening.

"We're as near war as we ever have been," said Olive's fiancé that evening. "Japan can't very well back down now, with her present militarist government."

Again, in the diary:

"December 2nd — The Japanese now want to resume talks with U.S. until 'the last moment', the suggestions are that they MUST continue talks for two weeks — by which time their war preparations will be complete."

"December 4th — The battleship *Prince of Wales* and more fleet is in Singapore. It is supposed/hoped it'll help the Japanese to change their minds, though 'Hull Hints Hope Abandoned' says the evening paper: I can't believe that."

"December 5th — Japan's reply is expected to be against U.S. policy, and which would mean breaking off diplomatic relations, then Japan going her own way re Indo-China and Burma Road, then war."

How so many of us (particularly those with children) could possibly have lived in such an atmosphere of inevitability without packing our cases and begging passages on the next ship out, I now just cannot imagine! I suppose we were partly mesmerised by the normalcy of life in the Colony in other ways. One would certainly never have guessed on Saturday 6th December that an attack was less then 48 hours away.

It was a race day, fine and sunny, bringing its usual crowds to Happy Valley. Arthur, in from the New Territories on a day's leave, took Barbara to the cinema to see *My Life with Caroline* and a newsreel showing comforting numbers of U.S. planes in formidable formation which would surely deter any would-be attacker!

The next morning, Mabel's boyfriend called, as he had managed a day off. We all decided to spend the afternoon at Repulse Bay beach, so Mabel and Sidney went into town to buy picnic foods. (Yes, many shops stayed open on Sundays in Hong Kong). Just after they left, another friend rushed in with the news that the Hong Kong Volunteer Defence Corps was mobilised, and all regular troops being recalled to barracks. Mabel and Sidney returned hotfoot soon after; a military policeman had stopped Sidney who was in uniform and told him to report to his unit. Sidney phoned his HQ and received confirmation of the order, so set off for the New Territories.

Yet the rest of us still continued to act our parts as distant observers of impending disaster rather than participants. Although the picnic was called off, we went to a nearby club and played tennis, rounding the day off with dinner at a friend's house. Though uneasy, we still had hope, as witness the domestic theme at the end of Barbara's diary for that day:

"I shall have to have something done about my teeth soon — back one is aching now. Finished knitting one of Arthur's bedsocks but am afraid it is too narrow."

The second bedsock was destined never to be finished.

★ ★ ★

The next day was Monday 8th December 1941.

We were awakened at 6.30a.m. by the front doorbell. A Chinese clerk from Barbara's office handed in a note telling her to report for duty at 7am. We knew this must mean that the political situation had worsened, and all dressed quickly. After Barbara had left we heard the first air raid sirens and the drone of planes.

"Here come the Japs, I think," Mabel shouted from the verandah. The distant thud of bombs provided instant confirmation — this was the Emergency at last. Olive hurried off to her office (Food Control), and Mabel to her army job, both in the city centre.

I knew that baby Jean's father had long ago made arrangements for the child to be cared for by a family friend in the event of war, as he knew I was committed to hospital duties. I telephoned him and he said he was sure this was the beginning of a full-scale attack; he was just about to leave home for his wartime post, and asked if I could spare an hour before reporting to my post to come and supervise the packing of the baby's clothing and paraphernalia and take her to his friends.

I made a hurried journey to his flat, got Jean and her luggage ready with the help of her amah, and we all left by taxi. Then I went home to get into uniform, advising our amah to remain indoors as much as possible. By now, everything was springing to life; auxiliary nurses, air raid wardens, uniformed volunteers and countless military lorries filled the streets, convincing us (although we still had had no announcements or instructions) that this was the real thing.

When I reached the Jockey Club, several of my colleagues were already there, and lorries with beds and medical equipment were arriving. We soon got the beds set up and the hospital in working order — thanks to the exercise of the previous week. The main betting hall became the male ward; the first floor was to be used for the operating theatre, doctors' and matron's rooms, and the female ward was on the top floor.

Soon our patients were brought in. They were all Chinese, and most were very old; they must have been mystified by all this activity. We bedded them down as rapidly as possible, but it was very difficult to get them warm, especially the men in the betting hall which had an open entrance at either end, and a third from the public enclosure in the centre. These entrances were partially sandbagged but the keen air swept into the ward nevertheless. We piled on more blankets, but what the patients really needed was hot food and this we could not yet give them.

With the patients from the Tung Wah Hospital came a large supply of bed linen, much of it soiled. It was sorted, and the dirty pile put in the garages against the time when it could be dealt with; but it never did get washed — life became too hectic to bother about clean sheets!

The Food Control Department had long since made plans for emergency feeding, and godowns (warehouses) all over the Colony were well stocked with food, but the suddenness of the attack and consequent congestion on the roads caused delays in deliveries. Eventually some sacks of rice arrived, but by the time we managed to get it cooked and distributed, the time was seven in the evening.

We ANS were allocated billets in a Chinese hotel at the far end of Happy Valley — about a five minutes' walk. We were told to go there in relays and book ourselves for a bed and meals. My neighbour Connie and I decided that as our flats were no further away than the hotel, we would continue to go home every evening, and have the comfort of our own beds and hot baths without having to queue — we still intended to have a comfortable war.

Air raids continued spasmodically during the day, though well away from our district. Later, some reconnaissance planes flew overhead. We discovered there was a military post next door to us in the Jockey Club Members' Enclosure, and once their guns got busy with AA fire, a few bombs were dropped in reply and fell on the opposite side of the race-course.

By evening things quietened down, and those of us who had finished duty left the hospital. Barbara came home to sleep, but the other two girls had been given billets near their offices in town. Barbara's diary for that day read:

"It's hardly worth writing, because I can't visualise us ever getting out of this, but I want to try to believe in a future."

It was a moonlight night and we expected more raids, but the only disturbances were two false siren alarms.

* * *

Back at the hospital the next morning I found that many casualties from the air raids had been brought in. Desultory planes continued to come over during the day, dropping propaganda leaflets as well as bombs. Vans were continuously bringing us supplies, and their drivers brought us messages from relatives and friends. We eagerly pressed all callers for news of what was happening in other parts of the Colony. They told of fierce fighting on the border and casualties among our forces. Some familiar names were mentioned, and it dawned on us that it would need more than the thrill of excitement to face up to what now seemed to be developing into war in earnest.

A load of clean bed linen arrived from the Tung Wah, so in between caring for the patients we sorted it and stacked it in the cupboards provided. There was so much of it that we were sure the war would be over long before we could use even half of it!

* * *

At home, our amahs were still managing to shop at the nearby markets so were always able to concoct some sort of meal for whoever dropped in at the flat. We left a writing pad on the table, and all callers left a note of their comings and goings, and any news items.

On the third day we heard that Mabel's boyfriend Sidney was a casualty in the Military Hospital. I had a few hours off so decided to visit him — no light undertaking as this hospital was several levels up the Peak and transport was at a premium and subject to frequent stoppages through air raids. I was on a tram, halfway to the city centre, when the siren sounded. The tram stopped, everyone got off and all but myself ran for the nearest cover. I could not face piling into a hillside tunnel with thousands of milling people whose language I could not speak. Instead, I hurried to the nearby RAOC depot and asked the sentry to let me in. After consulting his sergeant he did so, and I was led to shelter in a small doorway and left there. I looked about me, saw stout wooden boxes with rope handles piled from floor to ceiling, and realised I was in an ammunition store! I shot out of cover and ran after the sergeant, who took me to an underground shelter some distance away, and there I stayed until it was safe to resume my journey to the hospital.

Sidney was one of the first military casualties and had received a bullet wound through his shoulder while on reconnaissance with two others in the New Territories. Though not badly injured, he seemed very shocked and upset, because there was no news of his two colleagues.

I had just got back to our flat when planes droned overhead again; they could not be ours — we knew by now that the first day's raids on the airport had disposed of Hong Kong's meagre air force. Yet no siren had sounded, and there was just the hope that some RAF planes might fly up from Singapore, so I decided to go on the verandah and see what was happening. At that moment there was such a deafening crash of bombs that I was sure our block had been hit. The sound of glass from all the windows falling into the yard below was deafening, and the whole place filled with dust.

Ah Ding rushed in crying "O Missee, the kitchen has gone!" When the dust cleared we went along the passage to investigate and found the kitchen intact, although littered with broken dishes and all the window panes gone. The nearby Sikh Temple had caught the full force of the bombs, and many people sheltering there were killed.

We cleared up the debris in the flat as best we could. I could see Barbara's office from the verandah and it appeared to be intact. The young "makee-learn" amah had been out shopping during the raid; when she arrived back, terrified, I decreed that neither amah must go out again — we had plenty of dry and tinned foods to draw on.

When I returned to the hospital, the female patients were being moved down to the ground floor. Poor things, they had had a bad scare with the bombing so close at hand, and a direct hit on the Jockey Club would have annihilated them on the top floor. By moving the male patients up to one end and placing screens in the centre, we were able to accommodate the women in the betting hall.

Among our patients was a young girl expecting a baby any moment. A confinement in the midst of all this confusion was all we needed. The only privacy we could give her was a space between the wide concrete steps which, built in terraces, formed sitting accommodation outside for the racing spectators. The layette was hospital issue — tiny garments in harsh unbleached calico, as stiff as boards. One sympathetic soul washed them to try and soften them — luckily the baby did not arrive until they were dry.

When I met Barbara at home that evening, she said her unit had been told to sleep in the office until further notice. She begged me to arrange to sleep either at the hospital or the hotel. I argued that I would be quite all right in the flat with the amahs, but promised to go to the hotel if conditions worsened.

The next day — only the fourth of the war — came the disquieting news that the Japanese had penetrated the outskirts of Kowloon, and that our troops were hopelessly outnumbered and falling back all the time. We also heard — but scarcely believed — that the battleships *Prince of Wales* and *Repulse* had been sunk off Malaya. Feeling distinctly uneasy, Connie and I discussed the question of whether to return home to sleep that night, then decided to chance it. I was awakened by an unfamiliar noise — a terrific whistling followed by loud explosions. This heralded a new menace — shellfire, and could only mean that the enemy's ground force was getting nearer. Our guns began to return fire and the din was awful. The terrified amahs came running in to me, and we all spent the rest of the night in the sitting room, the amahs on the floor and me on the settee, Ah Ding insisting on putting a row of cushions on the floor alongside the settee in case I rolled off!

★   ★   ★

From the little bits of news that trickled into the hospital next day, it sounded as if the Japanese were now in full force in Kowloon, our troops having evacuated the mainland. Everyone was anxious about friends and relatives in Kowloon now it was completely in enemy hands. The hospital telephone was still functioning, though it was difficult to get a call through the overloaded lines. We gathered that most of the Europeans had escaped across the harbour as the Japanese moved in, but nurses and doctors had stayed in the hospitals. In the direct line of fire, theirs was a particularly grim slice of life until the battle ended.

We learned that the Japanese had mounted their heavy guns in godowns along the Kowloon seafront. Observers from the island could see them quite clearly, the harbour only being about a mile wide. (It was found later that gun platforms had been built in those godowns which had been leased to Japanese merchants before the war.) So our island was now at point-blank range.

Cut off as we were in Happy Valley, we really knew very little of exactly what was happening in other areas, though we were well aware that the Japanese were firing heavy guns in our direction. The shells were passing well above us, aimed at military posts up among the hills beyond, and Japanese planes circling round were evidently giving the range of these objectives.

More bombs were falling in our district. Barbara's office was now considered too vulnerable for an operational ARP HQ, and the staff transferred to the main Government office tunnel in town. She came home to pack a small suitcase and say goodbye. When she went off, I felt very desolate at the prospect of losing contact with all three girls under such uncertain conditions. It seemed incredible that only a week had passed since that glorious race day when the girls, their boyfriends and I had all been together.

With all the shelling and bombing, Connie and I decided that the time had come to take up our billets at the hotel. With three other ANS who also up to now had been sleeping at home, we presented ourselves there after duty that day. But now no beds were available for us; all we were offered was an opium divan to share. This was like a very wide settee of solid blackwood, with massive carved back and ends. It was a magnificent piece of furniture — the sort of thing used in the past by the wealthy for smoking opium. Three of us could have lain side by side lengthwise, but as there were five of us seeking accommodation, we had to settle for the short way, with our feet resting on chairs. I cannot imagine anything harder to lie on than a good solid piece of blackwood. Maybe in past days some Chinese had enjoyed their pipe dreams on this very couch, but for us there was not a wink of sleep; even if we could try to forget the hard bed, the continuous shelling kept us awake. Stiff in every joint, we all arose the next morning with the fixed determination to secure beds before going on duty.

We had only ourselves to blame for our bedlessness; not having booked in at the appointed time, our places had since been filled by other nurses who had joined our staff after their own posts had become untenable. Luckily, I met a girl who, being on night duty, said I was welcome to her bed when she was not using it, and the other four were able to make similar arrangements.

The shelling persisted all that day, many shells landing in the cemetery across the road from the Jockey Club. There was much activity among the military in the next enclosure — only the main entrance and lift shaft separated us. We often wondered whose bright idea it was to set up a military post complete with ack-ack guns under the same roof as a hospital. Now the military were moving out, and though there had been a certain comfort that some of our own soldiers were so near, we felt we were better off without them as they only drew fire on us.

It became increasingly difficult to get to the hotel for meals. All we could do was to wait for a lull in the battle, then make a dash for it. Once safely there, you made short work of the meal, then waited for the next lull to dash back to the hospital. This routine was based on one nurse's theory that there had to be a pause between bouts of shelling "to let the guns cool down". Whether this was fact or fiction we never knew, but it sounded feasible enough at the time to a group which had not the faintest idea of gunnery technique.

Connie's flat had been taken over by the Food Control Department as a distributing centre. Her amah came over to the hospital to report that the Food Control people were moving elsewhere, and Chinese coolies kept coming into the flat and helping themselves to the food stocks, so the amah had decided to bring some to Connie. She bravely made journey after journey with as much food as she could carry, as well as some of Connie's clothes. The last time she came she was terrified because looters were rampant and threatening. Connie got permission from Matron to let the amah stay at the hospital where she made herself very useful.

★   ★   ★

I had a message from Mabel. She had gone to visit Sidney in the Military Hospital and bumped into the Matron who demanded to know why she wasn't wearing the VAD uniform. "I'm not one of your nurses, Matron," Mabel replied, "but I would like to be."

She was accepted at once, Matron saying "We need all the nurses we can get." I felt less worried about her now, as the VADs had sleeping quarters in the hospital, so she would not need to leave the premises at all.

Hurrying in to the hotel that night, I was really looking forward to sleeping in a real bed after the previous night's ordeal, and was not even too put out on discovering that the billet I had been "lent" was actually a half-share of a double bed. My bedfellow turned out to be an attractive Continental ANS whom I knew slightly. Her husband had committed suicide several months earlier. She was very reserved, and her main worry seemed to be about her silver and other possessions which she had left in her room at the Gloucester Hotel in town. Although we only had a tiny blue lamp which gave practically no light, she began to go through the most elaborate beauty treatment before retiring. Attired in a gorgeous brocade housecoat, she stood before the mirror creaming and massaging her face. As we were on the top floor, the sound of the endless shells whining as they passed overhead was terrifying, and it seemed ludicrous to watch this woman going through all this beauty treatment when we were almost face to face with eternity.

We had not been long in bed when the heavy guns started up. The noise and flashes were so alarming that we decided it would be safer on a lower floor. Carrying a pillow each and our handbags, we groped our way down the dimly lit stairs. As we were unfamiliar with the layout of the hotel, we made for the only place we did know — the dining room on the first floor. Here we found the Chinese male staff in possession; some were stretched out across the tables, others squatting around smoking. They were surprised and amused to see us appear. One grinned and asked "Too muchee boom-boom, missies?" He then kindly pushed some tables together and indicated that we use them as beds.

Gratefully, we climbed up and settled ourselves, but with no thought of sleep. The glow of the boys' cigarettes, together with the dim light of two small blue lamps, lent an air of unreality. We could still hear the guns, but felt less vulnerable than on the top floor. After an hour or so we were nearly suffocated with the tobacco fug, so as soon as the noise outside had lessened, we wended our way back up the stairs and sank thankfully into the bed. But not for long: the shelling started again, the flashes lighting up our shaded room, the din appalling. We debated what to do. I was for remaining in bed and taking whatever was to come, for as things were I felt that we could hardly survive this lot — and I was so desperately tired. Suddenly my bedmate said: "Good job my husband shot himself." I hardly knew what to say to this peculiar remark, but before I could think of anything suitable, she went on, "He would have done it tonight, anyway: he couldn't have stood this."

Soon we both found that we couldn't stand it either, so crept downstairs again. The boys thought it a huge joke — perhaps it was as well we couldn't understand the conversation among them, as I can't imagine it was very flattering to us! In due course things quietened down again, and back upstairs we plodded, to sleep from sheer exhaustion until daylight.

Food supplies were getting low everywhere, so we were only able to have toast and jam for breakfast before going to the hospital. After that terrifying night, most of us decided to move into the hospital for keeps; no one wanted to risk their lives on that strip of road now that the lulls between shelling were getting shorter. There were plenty of spare camp beds, we each erected one in the betting booths near the patients, the heads pointing towards Kowloon, thus between us and the shells we had the protection of the underside of the concrete seating gallery outside. There was a gangway between each bed, and we also ended up with a very narrow gangway between the foot of the beds and the counters at which the shroffs used to sit to collect the betting money in palmier days.

That night brought more disturbance, not only from the shelling, but also from the patients who were groaning pitifully with pain and fright.

★　★　★

Next morning I was due a few hours off, so decided to risk a quick trip to our flat to see how the amahs were faring. Just as I was about to leave the hospital there came a heavy bout of shelling followed by an air raid, and bombs fell nearby. When the raid was over I ventured out, and saw more horror in that short journey home than I could ever have imagined. On open ground, directly opposite our block of flats, a food kitchen had been set up for distribution of food to the general public. The bombs had massacred the large queue waiting for their food. I had to step over mutilated bodies which were strewn all over the road and pavement — the poor victims had no chance against that unexpected onslaught.

At home the amahs were terrified. I had always assured them that the Japanese would never get into Hong Kong; but now we were besieged and under direct attack, I dared not bolster up that belief. Again I begged them to stay indoors, and said that if the Japanese did come, they must do what they were told to save themselves from any trouble.

"I might not be able to come home again until the war is over," I added with as much confidence as I could muster, "but I'll come back as soon as I can."

I gathered up a few clothes and some tins of food, and a large coloured photograph of the girls in a silver frame — their present to Will and me on our silver wedding the previous year, and the only item I now possess of our original home. The young amah wanted to carry the suitcase across to the hospital for me, but I could not allow this, fearing she might get injured and I would not know if she had got back home safely. Unable to face the terrible carnage on the front pavements, I left by the back door.

A plane came zooming overhead when I reached the paddock. I rushed to shelter in the first entrance to the Jockey Club, reaching there just as a small car drew up out of which hurried a nursing sister and a doctor. While we sheltered there we discussed the shell bombardment. This doctor was new to our hospital and I mentioned that we had had a direct hit and several near misses. The doctor was inclined to pooh-pooh the idea that the Japanese would attack the hospital as they were "fighting a gentleman's war". He insisted that any damage we sustained was just bad markmanship.

Presently, however, he was able to see for himself the damage that the lift and stairs had received from shells, and the wreckage of the upstairs rooms. Stocks of rattan chairs, which had been piled on the verandah overlooking the main road, had been blown across and scattered over the graves in the cemetery opposite.

The doctor suggested we get a large Red Cross flag made and display it without delay, since the small red cross painted on the roof did not appear to have been noticed, so that afternoon a flag was hurriedly made from a sheet and a piece of red blanket. The more difficult task was to get it hung in a conspicuous place. At last two of the Chinese boys were brave enough to make the attempt, and they managed to fit the flag on the wooden framework which normally carried boards with the names of the horses and riders in the races. But still there was no let up in the shelling, though we could hardly blame the enemy for refusing to believe that a hospital could suddenly appear where AA guns had hitherto been in action.

I heard that a Naval friend of the family — he had been in Shotley with us — had been killed by blast and was to be buried that afternoon. Not daring to venture out to the cemetery, I watched sadly from the hospital entrance when a naval van arrived with four coffins, one of which was our friend's, and thought of his wife and young son in Australia who would have to bear his loss. He had been a tower of strength to the girls and me when we returned from Manila and had to vacate our quarters, taking all four of us into his flat to stay until we found our own accommodation. Because of his connection with Will I was doubly distressed.

Miraculously, our phone was still working spasmodically. For days we had not been able to contact the sanitary authorities to collect our dead patients whose bodies were piling up in the garage behind the hospital — the routine established in the first few days whereby a sanitary lorry called daily to remove corpses had collapsed under the chaotic road conditions.

I managed to get Barbara on the phone one day. She and Olive usually managed to meet once a day as their offices were not far apart. Sidney had recovered from his wound and had now rejoined his regiment in the field. Mabel remained at the Military Hospital and was enjoying nursing. Barbara had forsaken her town billet where (like me) she had occupied a night-duty colleague's camp bed, and was now spending the nights with Peggy, another colleague in her flat on Macdonnell Road, part way up the Peak facing the harbour. This entailed a walk on shell-holed roads and steps morning and evening, but she thought the effort worth the comfort of a real home and bed at the end of the day. When she added that the previous evening she and Peggy had stood on the verandah and watched shells exploding in the Naval Dockyard some 500 yards below them, I was horrified and persuaded her to return to the town billet. Of course, anxiety for the girls was in the back of my mind all the time but, like everyone else, my days were too action-packed to give me much time to dwell on these worries.

Now, one day was very much like another. It was just a matter of trying to keep the patients as clean and comfortable as possible, and feeding them when meals could be prepared. No more supplies of any sort were getting through to us now, so food was rapidly becoming a major problem.

Apart from the continuing influx of casualties, our staff had been augmented by members of other units who, having had to evacuate their posts, had moved in with us. There was a fairly good stock of rice, but precious little else. The original kitchen — on the roof of all places — was no longer usable through shelling, and a makeshift one had been set up on the first floor, its window facing the race-course, so the risk of catching a stray shell made cooking a hazardous job. The only cookers here were just native chatties, which were familiar enough to the Chinese boys and amahs who would normally be doing the cooking for the hospital, but most of them had had to leave to look after their own families, so it was left to us nurses to cook as best we could with cookers we had never used before. Sometimes the rice was only half-cooked, sometimes burnt, but with a few beans from tins, it made a meal of sorts for those patients who were well enough to eat. The hospital tinned foods and Connie's supplies, which had seemed so plentiful a week before, were diminishing alarmingly and strict rationing was necessary.

Water was another problem. We had to get all our supplies from the washroom across the yard facing the racecourse. Here too were the toilets, and you took your life in your hands every time you left the shelter of the building.

Now casualties were being brought in hourly, many of them beyond aid. Particularly heart-rending was the case of a little Chinese boy with both arms severed below the elbows, and a man who had had both legs broken — he developed lockjaw and slowly starved to death. A young woman in labour was led in by her mother and brother who hung about the ward during the confinement. When the baby arrived I informed the brother, who could speak a little English. "Does the baby look Scotch?" he asked, explaining that the father was a corporal of the Royal Scots Regiment.

Another casualty brought to us was a corporal in the Middlesex Regiment. As we were a civilian hospital he should have been transferred to the Military Hospital. We managed to contact the Military Authorities by phone and were told he would be collected when a van could get through to us. So Tom stayed in his uniform, ready for instant departure. Our doctor tended his wounds — one in the shoulder and one in the leg — and we cleaned him up, but after three days he was still with us. We then persuaded him to change his uniform for hospital clothing, little thinking that this action would save his life. His uniform was bundled under his bed, in readiness for the Army lorry he insisted would be coming for him any minute.

A more unusual casualty was a large spaniel, Floss. Her owner was a nursing sister who had brought Floss and a second dog with her when moving into a billet near the Jockey Club. When the war situation made it unsafe to make even the shortest journey outside, the sister arranged for a policeman to shoot the dogs. Next day, anxious to satisfy herself that the animals were properly out of their misery, she dashed back to the billet. One dog was dead but Floss very much alive. She had thick long hair and the bullet had simply passed through the loose skin at her throat; she wheezed as she breathed but was otherwise untroubled, even though she was expecting a litter; Sister had no choice but to bring her back to the hospital with her,

★　★　★

What cheered us most during these steadily worsening days were frequent visits from a young Methodist minister. He often brought personal messages from our relatives and friends, and filled us in with the latest news — and very grim it was. On the 19th December, Japanese troops had landed on the island at a point about three miles from our hospital. Although we were assured that the invaders had been successfully mopped up, it was deeply disturbing to know that landings had even been possible. Now the minister had not called for three days, and it seemed we were completely cut off. Our senior doctor had gone into town on business two days earlier, and was never able to get back. We were left with two young Chinese doctors who told us they had had very little practical experience.

So here we were with a hospital full of badly wounded patients, little food and difficulty in getting water. We had salvaged what we could in the way of bandages when things had been quiet enough to risk going upstairs to the store, but shelling had by now reduced even the store to a shambles, so we were having to cut off the soiled parts of used bandages and dressings and re-use the remainder. We toyed with the idea of going up to the remains of the original roof kitchen to see if there was any tinned food to salvage, but Matron forbade it because of the exposure to shellfire there.

A very sketchy diary I kept says:

"December 22nd — Breakfast — bacon and bread."

The bacon I had brought from home on my final visit, and cooking it was a real adventure: it was a matter of dashing into the vulnerable kitchen and hurriedly scorching it up (before the next shell was due over) in a dented saucepan on a chatty.

The diary continues: "Tiffin — nil."

The times of meals now depended on when we could get food cooked, and that in turn depended on whether the enemy was firing in our direction.

"December 23rd — Breakfast — toast and jam." (This should read "scorched bread and jam" — we had a lot to learn about the art of toasting on a chatty, but the bread was several days old and would have been inedible without some disguise.)

Tiffin that day was "meat paste from a tin".

★　★　★

To our great delight, our friend the minister turned up again that day, bringing among letters and packages a parcel for me from Olive and Barbara — some very welcome bars of chocolate. He told us that our forces were holding their own against the invading Japanese. Bidding us to keep our chins up, he left and we never saw him again; later we learned that on his return journey he was wounded by shellfire and succumbed to his injuries.

During the afternoon, when things seemed quieter, we cooked some rice for the patients, then were told to go to the kitchen in relays to have some ourselves with a small portion of corned beef. The first "sitting" had just started when a burst of rifle fire shattered the kitchen window and splintered glass flew all over the place. Luckily no one was hit, but the precious food was ruined, and we had to content ourselves with tinned tongue and baked beans, eaten with our fingers downstairs in the ward.

The rifle fire evidently came from snipers across the valley in the Leighton Hill area, so the enemy were much nearer than we had dreamed. This sniping continued and now we hardly dared cross the yard to use the toilets or empty bedpans. Some brave souls who did venture out found that the water supply had failed completely. This was real disaster. (We did not know then that the Japanese had captured the reservoirs and cut off all water supplies.) All we had left was a small galvanised bin of drinking water, and an emergency tank of water which we could not use as the key was in the pocket of a Chinese doctor who had gone to town and not returned. Washing patients and ourselves was out, but one nurse produced a large bottle of eau de cologne and let us each have a spot on a piece of toilet paper to wipe over our faces as a freshener.

Grim though things were, there was one bright spot to that day; one of the nurses who was standing at the end of the ward near the entrance suddenly pointed through the gap between the sandbags and cried, "Look, that coolie is wearing my hat!"

We followed her gaze: sure enough, there were two coolies carrying a large sack between them, and on the head of one, at a rakish angle, sat our colleague's hat, which had been hanging upstairs in the cloakroom. With one accord, a group of us made a dash at the men, who dropped the sack and took to their heels. Their loot turned out to be tinned goods and minerals, which we guessed must have been taken from the adjacent evacuated Army post. We hadn't imagined that the military had left anything worth having behind them, else we might have investigated earlier. The sack of food was a godsend to us, and we decided to risk a visit to the post to see if there was any more. We had not been up there since the shell had wrecked the lift, but we thought that if the looters could manage to get up there, so could we. There was plenty of food left, and what is more, the looters had kindly collected it all into one pile and stacked it in one of the rooms over the hospital section of the building. No doubt their idea was to remove it gradually. We took down as much as we could carry on one trip, still leaving plenty for the coolies should they come back. We didn't dare make a second journey just in case we should encounter more looters who might turn nasty. Several coats had vanished from the adjacent cloakroom too, so there had obviously been earlier visits. Anyway, we had replenished our larder, thanks to the coolie who could not resist fine feathers.

★　★　★

We began to realise that things were not going well in the field when a row of Government houses on Leighton Hill (about 500 yards from the Jockey Club) were set on fire that night. It was a fearsome sight to see the homes of people we knew going up in flames. One of our ANS lived there, and I will never forget the look of blank misery on her face as she watched her home being destroyed.

Next morning, the 24th December, we ate the last of the bread with jam and the luxury of half a bottle of mineral water each. For tiffin we had meat paste and cold rice, not daring to be too extravagant with the newly acquired tinned food as there was no way of knowing how long it would have to last. When the cooked rice ran out there could be no more as there was no water to cook in.

Two members of another unit which had been evacuated came in to the Jockey Club and told us that the Japanese had made a landing at North Point — a couple of miles from us. Still we did not worry unduly on that score, as we had understood earlier that the Royal Scots had gathered at that point after their evacuation from Kowloon. Little did we know that the

Royal Scots had suffered heavy casualties and were withdrawing back into town.

As there was a strict blackout, we had to attend to the patients while it was still daylight. There was not much we could do for them now, anyway — washing them was out of the question, even cleansing their wounds was difficult as we had come to the end of the bandages. For some of the worst cases, we ripped up some old sheets to use as dressings and bandages. No chance of sterilising anything now!

In all this grimness, this was the stage at which Connie reminded us that it was Christmas Eve . . .

We listened tensely as the firing continued, every minute expecting an onslaught of enemy troops on our post . . . then we gradually realised that the firing was receding in the direction of the city. All we could think of now was how our dear ones would fare with a full-scale battle raging in the crowded streets. That night dragged interminably. I thought of last Christmas when we entertained the girls' boyfriends and several lonely husbands of evacuated wives to dinner. Although there was no chance of sleep, there was no desire for conversation. I think we were all afraid to talk for fear of triggering off the emotions of the more nervous (not that any of us felt very brave).

Morning came at last, and we rose with grim set faces, knowing without doubt that this Christmas Day was going to be as none other had ever been. Those of us on morning duty walked to the sandbagged entrance to take a few breaths of fresh air. A mist hung over the racecourse, adding an air of unreality to this period of waiting to see what happened next. Dr Selby, a Scottish doctor who had joined us from an evacuated post the previous day, appeared from the yard.

"Well, that's that," he said. It seemed he had persuaded some of the few remaining Chinese boys to help him dig shallow graves on the racecourse to dispose of the pile of putrefying bodies in the garage. It was a great comfort to us ANS to have a European man around — the only other was Tom, the soldier, who had never been collected by the RAMC — for our one thought now was that the Japanese would take over the hospital before long.

Someone suddenly realised that things might go badly with Tom and ourselves if the Japanese found a soldier in a civilian hospital, so we hurriedly pulled his uniform from beneath his bed and stuffed it down behind a huge stack of wooden chairs at one end of the building. Luckily, Tom's rifle and hand grenades had been handed over to the Military Post which had still been functioning next door at the time he was brought to us.

With the doctor, we considered our water problem. He suggested we collect some in cans from the remaining water in the base of a large fountain in the cemetery across the road, as this water could at least be used for washing. We were preparing to do this when an astonishing sight met our eyes: an Anglo-Indian doctor, well known in the Colony, came through the entrance; his hands were tied behind his back and he was propelled by several Japanese soldiers who held a rope attached to his hands. The party advanced down the hall towards us, the soldiers dwarfed by their tall hostage. They were draped in netting with greenery stuck in the mesh as camouflage. With bayonets and rifles at the ready, they halted. One, holding a revolver, stepped forward. Dr Selby placed himself in front of us and faced him. The Japanese gazed around at the patients and said, "Oh, hospital?"

Dr Selby confirmed this.

"You doctor?"

"Yes."

Motioning to him to put his hands up, the Japanese went through all Dr Selby's pockets, scanning letters and papers then throwing everything to the floor. Next he directed the doctor over to the table in the centre of the ward where the hospital records were kept — although we had long since given up keeping them. He scrutinised each paper in turn, casting them to the floor as he finished them. He then carried on a subdued conversation with the doctor in stilted English.

Meanwhile we nurses just stood where we were, the soldiers regarding us with curious toothy grins. A more unprepossessing lot one could not imagine — dirty, unkempt and unshaven. I suppose their condition was excusable as they had been fighting for days, and no doubt we ourselves didn't look any too spruce by normal standards.

Dr Selby was brought back to us, still covered by the officer's revolver, and told us we were now prisoners of the Japanese and must not try to leave the building; we must remain here and look after the sick people, and do as we were told.

"I'm not able to stay with you," he ended, "but have courage and carry on with your duties."

Matron reminded him of the water difficulty before he was led away, so he asked the Japanese for permission for us to go to the cemetery to get some. Permission was given, so gathering up every available pail and jug, about half a dozen of us hurried through the main entrance. Here we encountered two Japanese sentries who lunged at us with fixed bayonets and halted us.

One brave soul dangled her bucket aloft and said, "We want to get water — plenty sick people."

The bucket did not impress the soldier, but the nurse's rings did: making her drop the bucket, one relieved her of her rings and a gold wristwatch. Both then systematically inspected us all and demanded our valuables, chanting, "Gold for Japan." Those with platinum rings were lucky as the Japanese didn't want them, nor did they want my chromium watch. But I had to hand over my wedding ring, and they also demanded Will's ring which I had worn ever since his death. I pretended it was too tight to get off, but a bayonet pointed uncomfortably near my stomach quickly made me change my mind. Pocketing their spoils, the sentries motioned us to go and get the water.

We crossed the road to the cemetery gate. It was locked, so the more agile nurses started to climb over it. Immediately, bullets began to fly from the direction of the cemetery, zipping against the wall of the hospital now behind us. Evidently there were snipers among the tombstones up in the terraces in the cemetery. We all dashed back to the hospital entrance to shelter, and were greeted with great hilarity by the sentries who had been watching us. Possibly whoever was doing the shooting only meant to scare us as, had they wanted, they could have picked us all off very easily. Anyway, we decided that water would have to remain a problem a little longer.

★ ★ ★

Back in the hospital the atmosphere was very tense now that Dr Selby had been taken away. Every so often little groups of Japanese soldiers would come and just gape at us. I suppose the sight of white women prisoners was quite a novelty.

Our camp beds had been spread out over the two largest betting booths, but now Matron advised us all to move into the one booth so, as unobtrusively as possible, between the visitations of the soldiers, we jammed all our beds hard up against each other. Also at Matron's direction, we sat or stood round the long tables in the centre of the ward and busied ourselves tearing up sheets and mattress covers into bandage lengths and rolling them. Any idea of getting together a meal for ourselves or the patients seemed out of the question. We hardly dare speak to each other for fear of giving way. It would only need one to break down to set us all off, as not only were our thoughts on our own safety but also that of our relatives and friends elsewhere in the Colony.

Presently, in trooped a large party of very scruffy soldiers, armed to the teeth and looking very pleased with themselves. They stood around and surveyed us all, conversing animatedly. The strain for us was horrible. At last they moved off through the building. Some time later, one of the few remaining Chinese ward boys came running in to say that soldiers were raping the young Chinese girls belonging to St John Ambulance Brigade who had sought refuge with us several days earlier. There was nothing we could do, except to try and comfort the poor girls when they came in to us, crying their hearts out and badly shocked.

So Christmas Day wore on, with intermittent visits from small groups of soldiers who watched us curiously. Excepting for occasional attention to some pain-racked patient, there was little we could do but continue the bandage-rolling. The materials to hand were almost all used up so we had to go slow on the job in order to keep ourselves and our minds occupied. Soft conversation gradually resumed among us. Connie was making a stock of swabs with the only remaining roll of cotton wool. When the roll was finished, she painstakingly re-rolled the swabs over and over again.

"They'll make good hand grenades if I roll these things much more," she muttered.

When a heavily armed party of soldiers drifted in, she whispered "Just look at them! They've got everything on but the kitchen sink."

But this was no time for jokes, and someone promptly hissed her into silence. One of this new mob

114

appeared to be drunk and was waving his revolver about in an alarming manner. He leaned over the table between two of the nurses and jabbered Japanese to them in maudlin tones. Some of his companions tried to coax him away from us, but this seemed to anger him. Just then, Dr Selby re-appeared, escorted by an armed guard. He was allowed to speak to us for a moment.

"Keep your chins up," he said. He himself looked drawn and anxious.

The drunken soldier rushed over to him, still brandishing the revolver; then, taking the doctor's hand and resting his other hand with the gun on the doctor's shoulder, he proceeded to dance with him, grinning the while. Dr Selby carefully waltzed him away from us up to the far end of the ward. Here stood a trolley with the usual hospital paraphernalia. This seemed to interest the soldier, who stopped to investigate. He then made signs on his wrist with his forefinger to indicate that he wanted an injection. To satisfy him, Dr Selby quickly took a syringe and gave the soldier an injection — of what, we did not know, but he seemed well pleased with himself and went off quietly with his companions. Our doctor was led away again.

We had noticed that the Japanese were very friendly towards two of our Chinese patients — shell victims who were only slightly injured. The soldiers brought them cigarettes and biscuits, and presented them with khaki drill caps such as they themselves wore. These two patients proudly donned them and, though in bed, wore them from then on. We considered them to be fifth columnists.

We were very wary of another patient from the moment he was first brought in to the hospital. He looked more Japanese than Chinese, and lay on his bed, smoking continuously, assuring us in perfect English that he had influential friends who would get him taken elsewhere for medical attention. He refused to put on hospital clothing and insisted on wearing his excellent quality overcoat all the time. Immediately the Japanese walked into the hospital, he was on very good terms with them, and conversed freely with them in Japanese.

Our soldier Tom had been admitted before all three suspect fifth columnists, so we hoped they did not know he was a British soldier. So fearful were we that he would be discovered that we smothered him with blankets and warned him not to show his face. Luckily he was very dark-haired, but we felt very nervous on his behalf every time soldiers sauntered into the ward.

Reluctant as we were to move about unnecessarily in the presence of our captors, in the early afternoon hunger drove us to rustle up some kind of a meal — our first that day. A few tins of meat and beans were opened and shared around. A handful of food was passed under the blanket to Tom, and some water in a feeding cup. No one's hunger was satisfied as the portions were meagre.

The afternoon dragged on. We resumed bandage rolling, although by this time all the available material had been cut and rolled, but we felt a compulsion to appear busy whenever soldiers passed through, so kept dropping the bandages to have the excuse to re-roll them. The heavy shelling had stopped, although planes were still around. There was a sense of the whole world standing waiting for we knew not what.

In the middle of the afternoon there sounded what we thought was a long-drawn roll of thunder, followed by further rumbles. This seemed as strange as everything else that was happening to us, for the bright sunshiny weather was anything but thundery. What a good thing for our taut nerves that we never dreamed the truth: our own guns were being destroyed before surrender to the enemy.

Came the evening, and although no thoughts were voiced, the strained look on each of our faces spoke of the dread of the night hours. We made the patients as comfortable as possible, and when the night staff took over the rest of us retired into the unlit sleeping booth.

Many of the younger girls, nervous of the way the soldiers had eyed them during the day, made up beds for themselves by spreading blankets underneath the counters. Some even crawled beneath the low-slung camp beds with blankets, prepared to spend the night there, despite the concrete floor beneath.

Presently we heard ribald singing from the next enclosure — our captors were making merry. We lay listening and wondering, but never guessing that the Japanese were celebrating the surrender of our forces. Suddenly the beam of a powerful torch appeared at the ward entrance. We could see it from where we lay because our booth had only half swing doors through to the ward. A group of soldiers shone their way to the beds where the two coolie fifth columnists lay. There was much jocular conversation among them all, then the torch flashed round the booth and we huddled beneath our blankets.

"Get up all," commanded one of the soldiers. Two carried bayonets and rifles, the others were unarmed.

We scrambled up as best we could — getting out from a camp bed by way of the foot is not something one can do with dignity — and stood in a line. The girls on the floor kept perfectly still, hoping not to be noticed. The Japanese pushed their way along the narrow gap between us and the tables, scrutinising each of us in turn as they shone the light in our faces. It was a terrible ordeal. One of my near neighbours was the attractive widow with whom I had shared a bed in the small hotel: her eyes flashed defiance, she looked like a wild animal at bay, and I prayed she would do nothing to anger these uncouth men, as I felt sure she would claw at them if they made any advances to her, but they passed her by. Four of the younger girls were selected to accompany the soldiers back to their quarters, with the threat: "Go Jap — no come, kill all!"

They went off with the terrified sobbing girls, commanding the rest of us, "Sleep!"

We got miserably back into our beds, not daring to talk, stunned as we realised how completely we were at our captors' mercy.

At length the poor girls came running back in great distress. Before we could try to comfort them, the soldiers returned. This time they did not make us all get up, but just went from bed to bed shining the torch on each occupant. Then they flashed the torches under the counters and saw the girls huddled there and ordered them out. Again they made a selection and, with the same threat as before, forced them to go off with them. None dared refuse lest we should all be slaughtered. Once more we were left in darkness.

Presently I felt a movement under my bed and a voice whispered, "Can I get in with you? I'm so cold."

There was really no room but somehow the owner of the voice, fortunately very small and thin, managed to squeeze in beside me. She said her name was Pat. She was a school teacher who had joined us halfway through the battle when her post was evacuated. I only knew her by sight.

"Don't let them get me," she pleaded.

How I could stop them, I could not think. I said if the soldiers came again, she must wriggle right down in the bed and keep very close to me; perhaps with my bulk she might not be noticeable, especially as I had my heavy coat on top of the blankets. Pat did not wait for the next visitation, she dived down right away and I was afraid she would suffocate. She said she had got so stiff with the cold that she just had to come out from under the bed while she could still move. She was not discovered when the soldiers returned for more victims, nor were any of the girls hiding beneath the beds discovered — the beds being so low and so tightly jammed together that there was not even space for the soldiers to get down and look.

A young married woman who was taken away became hysterical and fainted in the ward, and the soldier dragged her back to her bed. One stalwart nurse bravely snatched the torch from the soldier to search the medical trolley for something to revive the girl. She motioned to the soldier to bring the large bottle of boracid lotion; he obediently did so, and using this in lieu of water she managed to bring the girl round. The soldier seemed rather worried by this turn of events, and as soon as he got his torch back, departed alone.

Again we waited for the return of the latest victims. It was harrowing for us older women as well as for the victims; we could only witness their distress without being able to lift a finger to help them, and those of us (like me) who had daughters elsewhere in the Colony could only hope and pray they were not being treated in the same way. The night seemed endless, but at last things quietened down; the singing ceased and, we dared to hope, the visitations.

"Do you think they'll come again?" whispered Pat.

"No, I should think they've settled down for the night," I said hopefully.

She began to get up, saying, "I can't stay here." Thinking she meant to crawl back beneath my bed, I tried to persuade her to spend what was left of the night in the warm with me, but she insisted on clambering out and disappeared in the darkness.

* * *

Morning came, but glad as we were to see daylight once more, we faced it with terrible misgivings, knowing now what to expect from the enemy. Several soldiers walked through the ward, all seeming very jubilant. Through the gaps in the sandbags at the entrance facing the racecourse, we could see numbers of small ponies lined up on the grass, so realised the Japanese had landed quite freely in large numbers. The fact that they could transport not only themselves but also their ponies, seemed ominous, yet although we could hear no gunfire, it still did not dawn on us that they were now in complete possession of the Colony.

Hollow-eyed and drawn, we went our rounds as usual, doling out sips of precious water and giving what ease we could to the patients. Connie had some surprising news about my bedfellow of the previous night; it seemed Pat had borrowed a spare Chinese suit from Connie's amah and escaped from the hospital in the dark.

"She's taken an awful risk," said Connie. "She must have plenty of guts."

It was another trying morning, each of us trying to keep occupied doing nothing in particular; the only job we could do was take the used bedpans out to the lavatories to empty without fear of being shelled.

Towards midday, for the sake of something to do, several of us went into the booth where the remains of the bed linen was stored, and began — quite unnecessarily — to re-stack it. In rushed one of the girls who had been raped during the night, crying, "Hide me, quickly!" Before we could do so, a dishevelled soldier ran in and grabbed her, saying, "Go Jap." She tried to cling to me, crying piteously. I motioned to the soldier to release her, saying, "No can, plenty work to do." But he dragged her away, and they were halfway down the ward when there was a sudden shout from the entrance. He let go of the girl and dashed away. Released, she ran back to us. Then we saw why — a group of officials were into the ward. We recognised, with overwhelming relief, our Director of Medical Services, Dr Selwyn-Clarke, with another European and two Japanese officers. They went over to our Matron, to whom the DMS introduced the Japanese who bowed politely. One of the Japanese then announced that the war was over; we were all friends now, etc. etc.

But our Matron was not interested in flowery speeches. Calmly addressing herself to the DMS, she asked that we be removed from the hospital forthwith. The DMS said there had been fantastic tales of the happenings here from some hysterical woman, and they had come to investigate. Matron told him there was no fantasy about what had happened: the behaviour of the soldiers towards the nurses had been appalling and we must not be allowed to spend another night in the place. The DMS said he had already acted on the girl's report, having called on the Japanese Commandant who had said if we could identify the men who had robbed us of rings and watches, they would be duly punished. (What a hope — all the soldiers looked alike to us.)

By now, we realised that Pat's brave escape to report our plight to officialdom was the reason for our deliverance from more horrors. How relieved we were to know that she herself had come to no harm. The officials agreed that the whole post should be evacuated, we nurses to the Queen Mary Hospital, the patients to be distributed among two other hospitals. We were to accompany the patients and see them into their new places on our way to Queen Mary Hospital.

The DMS took away as many of the shocked rape victims as he could cram into his car, and the rest of us prepared ourselves and the patients for evacuation. Tom, the soldier patient, was still on our minds. Even though the war was now over, the Japanese were the victors and we could not be sure how they would react if he were to be discovered in a civilian hospital. Matron had the bright idea of disguising him as a European female patient who could therefore come with us to the Queen Mary. She bandaged his head, then over the bandage tied a piece of sheet that looked like a mob cap.

Around three in the afternoon the lorries arrived and off we went. The route out of Happy Valley ran past our flat in Gap Road. There were Japanese soldiers on our verandah. We could not hold back the tears at the sight of the devastation of so many familiar places. Detachments of Japanese soldiers were everywhere, and it was with a great feeling of relief when we saw the Queen Mary Hospital towering ahead of us and knew we would soon be among our own people.

Stale and unwashed for days, we were all dying for a bath — or even a wash, but gratefully sat down first for some tea that awaited us. The water supply had been restored here, so we each had a glorious bath; four to a room, we were accommodated in the Sisters' quarters adjacent to the hospital, and tumbled thankfully into bed, to drop into our first real sleep for weeks.

We were given the next day off to recuperate, and surprisingly, told that since hostilities were over, any of us who were able to do so could return to our homes and connect up with our families. Since few of us knew if our homes still existed, nor the whereabouts of our families, and in any case had no transport, the last thing we wanted to do was leave the security of the hospital after all we had been through, so we all stayed to continue nursing.

We spent the free day roaming about the quarters, asking everyone we met for news of relatives and friends. There was no way of finding out anything definite, but I did meet people who had seen both Olive and Barbara recently with their respective units. Mabel, as far as I knew, was still at the Military Hospital — I prayed so, as there was talk that some of the VADs had been sent to augment staff in a hospital at Stanley where there had been terrible happenings — many soldier patients and three nurses murdered.

We found out how Pat had fared after she left us on Christmas night. Almost invisible in the amah's black clothes, she had dodged across the road to the cemetery, the terraces of which extend up the hillside to the main road. Using the tombstones as cover, she safely reached the road, then walked nearly two miles to the military hospital which she reached, exhausted, in the early hours of the morning. She managed to convince the British sentry at the entrance that despite her disguise, she was English, and was taken to the

Army Medical Officer to whom she poured out the story of our plight. He took immediate steps to get the information to the DMS who contacted the Japanese Commandant, with the result that we were at least saved from another harrowing night.

★   ★   ★

Once back on duty in wards full of war casualties, both civilian and servicemen, our days were well filled, as many of the Chinese staff had left to fend for their families in this difficult situation. Tom, no longer disguised as a female, was in a ward with some of his buddies at last. It was harrowing to see so many young men, shattered not only by their wounds but also by their failure to withstand the onslaught of the enemy.

In addition to anxiety about relatives and friends, there was the ever-present question: what will the Japanese do with us now? Our soldiers seemed resigned to being shipped off to Japan as prisoners of war, but we knew of no precedent for the treatment of several hundreds of civilian prisoners. The Japanese were in and out of the hospital all day long making inspections, the officers clanking around in huge brown leather boots and trailing swords, some of which were fitted with a small wheel for ease of progress.

I fell ill and had a few days as a patient myself. When I returned to duty, many of the badly wounded were greatly improved, and their spirits revived. Now each was vying with the other in recounting the best stories of the various field actions they had been through.

Many of the casualties were Canadians, pathetically young, some having lied about their ages in order to join up. They had had little training before being drafted to Hong Kong, and their three weeks in the Colony before our war started had not been sufficient to familiarise them with the area. The brief war had taken a terrible toll of their ranks.

As transport began moving a little news began to trickle in of relatives and friends. The driver of a lorry from the Military Hospital brought me firsthand news of Mabel: she was safe and well; Sidney was at the hospital too, having been wounded a second time — he had lost the tops of two fingers. From another visitor I learned that Olive and Barbara were housed separately in small Chinese hotels with their units. We heard too that European women with young children had had a nightmare war. The plan in peacetime to congregate them in houses on the Peak had worked out badly, since the prominent Peak buildings proved vulnerable targets for shelling, and the unfortunate people had been shunted from one place to another in an effort to get somewhere safe.

At first we were very well fed at the Queen Mary Hospital, but after three weeks it began to be apparent that care must be taken of the supplies in hand as there was no sign of any more food forthcoming. It was even more of a problem outside the hospital. One day Connie saw a ward coolie hurrying through the ward with a covered bedpan. She watched him when she realised he was heading in the opposite direction to the sluice room. She ran after him and uncovered the pan

126

and found it full of rice! Another day, a nurse on an upper verandah noticed bundles of food being handed out of the ground floor kitchen window to a waiting recipient. A quick phone message to the kitchen put paid to that enterprise.

Rumours about our future came and went, but one gained ground: all civilians and service personnel were to be interned, civilians in Stanley, combatants to barracks on the island and in Kowloon. Our own hospital authorities had no idea when this would take place. In the event the Japanese gave us one day's notice. On January 19th they told us to have all naval and military patients ready for removal, the bedfast to the Military Hospital, the convalescent to Shamshuipo Barracks, Kowloon; we civilians were to go to Stanley the day after their removal.

Most of the servicemen had no clothes other than hospital pyjamas. Their uniforms were still where they had been piled when taken off them — there had been no chance to wash and cleanse them during the fighting; now, filthy and bloodstained, they were only fit for burning. We managed to rig the convalescent out with dressing-gowns, but there were not enough slippers to go round so many had to go barefoot.

The sick patients were moved on stretchers handled by coolies under Japanese supervision. One young sailor had a terrible arm injury on which he had an aeroplane splint, and we always had to handle him very gently. As the coolies came into his ward, he begged, "Don't let them touch me!" All I could think of was to ensure that he was the last patient to leave the ward, then I could leave with him and try to help him into the ambulance. When his turn came, I tried to support the splinted arm as the coolies went to lift him from bed to stretcher. The Japanese officer in attendance motioned the coolies aside, then, by signs, indicated that he and I would help to lift him. Never will I forget how tenderly he handled that patient and then escorted him to the lift.

The patients away, we could now think of our own departure. Internment was an unknown state to us all, and we just could not imagine what our living conditions would be like, but instinct told us to take with us everything we could possibly carry. The regular nursing staff who lived in adjacent quarters were able to select their internment wardrobes and chattels, but we auxiliaries had only the clothes we stood up in and a small suitcase apiece. We were delighted then, when once they had finished their packing, the Sisters told us to help ourselves to anything we fancied left in their rooms.

After living in dingy grey uniforms for so long, it was a real joy to handle nice clothes. In no time the Sisters' quarters resembled a dress store during a bargain sale, all of us clutching our newly acquired possessions and searching for more — and all for free! It was wonderful for morale. We were also allowed to raid the baggage room and take any of the remaining cases and baskets in which to carry off our spoils.

Matron, a woman of great foresight, decided we should take with us some spare mattresses from the storeroom, in case there were not enough beds to go round in Stanley. Since the storeroom was on the seventh floor and the lift was out of action as there was no electricity working, the only way to get the mattresses downstairs was to slide them one by one down the stairs from floor to floor; two girls were stationed on each landing (lit only by hurricane lamps) to turn the mattresses round and start them down the next flight. It was a back-breaking job, but we felt well pleased with ourselves when a goodly number were piled on the ground floor ready for internment with us. But alas, Matron had overlooked that she was no longer in sole charge of the hospital; next morning when the Japanese authorities saw what we had done, they refused to allow us to take the mattresses away — thank goodness they did not make us return them to the storeroom!

Trucks to take us to Stanley were due to come at midday, so we rushed around that morning, carrying baskets of food stocks intended for the future internment camp hospital, baskets of fresh vegetables from the hospital gardens, and of course our own belongings. Matron handed us each a few tins of food and some cutlery. How we regretted later that we had not helped ourselves more liberally to the useful things lying around! Looting was not part of our make-up, otherwise we would all have gone into camp better equipped with the little everyday things which we didn't miss until we found ourselves without them. I picked up an alarm clock and a small teapot as I went through the kitchen on my way out of the hospital, and both items proved their worth in due course.

When the trucks came we clambered aboard, dragging our luggage on as best we could. There followed the usual long wait associated with official arrangements all over the world. Someone had the excellent idea of using up all the remaining perishable foodstuffs in the kitchen, so while we sat perched on our luggage, we were handed thick cheese sandwiches, the hot midday sun (even in January) melting the butter which had been very generously spread. When and where we would get our next meal was beyond conjecture, so every mouthful was savoured.

After an hour or so, the sun on our bare heads became too much for us, so two of the Sisters went back to their quarters and collected all the hats and umbrellas they could find, and distributed them among us. I got a tricky little number in black velour with a broad satin bow — a very nice hat, but it must have looked ridiculous on me at the time.

At 2.30pm some Japanese officers arrived and ordered us off the lorries while our baggage was inspected. A couple of soldiers them mounted each lorry and to our exasperation, tumbled everything out of the cases and rummaged through our belongings. Containers that were roped or secured in any way soon yielded to a strong knife. They threw out such articles as rattan and other pieces of furniture which some Sisters had hopefully loaded, then directed us on to the lorries again to bundle our things back in the cases as best we could.

At last we were off, round the familiar coastal roads, but the picture postcard scenery was ignored, for the

Japanese driver occupied all our attention with his erratic driving. At times we feared we might be swept off the lorry by overhanging branches of trees at the roadside. My velour hat blew off, and the last I saw of it, it was being fought over by a couple of small Chinese urchins.

The Japanese flag was well in evidence at most of the little wayside stalls and dwellings we passed — more a matter of expediency than disloyalty, we thought, beginning to realise that our lives would no longer be our own, but regulated to whatever pattern our captors dictated.

There was little conversation among us on the five-mile journey, owing to the presence of a Japanese guard who might have understood a little English. Now, as we passed the grim gates of Stanley gaol (and how thankful we felt that we were not taken through them as we had feared), one of the girls whispered, "What now?"

Connie whispered back, "Cheer up girls! Whatever happens, it's only for three months, remember Winston said so." Three months did not sound too bad, but if at that moment we had been given the power to see not three months but more than three years stretching before us, we just could not have borne it.

CHAPTER
FIVE

When We Came to
Our Cuttings Down

The lorries stopped on waste ground beyond the gaol, almost at the water's edge. The guards grunted at us as a signal to us to climb off our perches. They threw our effects down after us, and seemed in a great hurry to get away, one lorry backing over the baskets of fresh vegetables and ruining the food.

The regular nursing staff and the few British civilian patients we had brought with us were directed to a three-storeyed red brick building within a stone's throw of the rocky shore. Pre-war this had been single men's quarters for the Indian staff of the gaol, but it had been equipped and used as an emergency hospital during hostilities and was known as Tweed Bay Hospital; it was now to serve the internment camp as its hospital — nurses on the top floor and patients on the ground and first floors.

We auxiliaries were sent to find accommodation for ourselves in the former staff European gaol staff quarters — a large block of cream-coloured three-storeyed flats built on high ground overlooking the gaol and some 200 yards from the hospital. Off we went, laden with our treasured belongings, up the steep ramp leading to the flats. Earlier arrivals from other parts of the Colony already in residence lined the green railings which surrounded the blocks, watching for friends and relatives to arrive. We asked if they could direct us to empty rooms.

"Rooms, did you say?" said one. "You'll be lucky if you can find a bedspace."

Thinking our best chance was to hunt in small numbers, Connie and I set off together. We poked our heads in every room we passed, asking if there were any spaces, but each seemed to have its full complement — some as many as eight in one room. We began to worry. It had been a long and tiring day. There was no one in charge to go for help, and we feared we would have to settle for the bare concrete floor in one of the entrance halls. Imagine our relief, then, when we came upon a large unoccupied room containing a table and a settee. I sank down on to the settee to guard our possessions while Connie dashed off to collect some of our colleagues to come and share our find. She had hardly left the room when I heard footsteps coming down the stairs from the flat above. A Chinese man walked in, and I don't know which of us was the more surprised to see the other.

"You go, missee," he said in some agitation. "This room belong Japanese. Plenty Japanese on top floor, soon they come here. Please you go quickly."

I lost no time in removing myself and luggage and trudged off to find Connie. (It transpired that the

Japanese had reserved that particular set of flats for their administrative staff, but they later moved to a bungalow some distance from our blocks which made us feel easier than having them on our doorstep.) When I met up with Connie she already had two of our colleagues in tow to share our prospective room; now all they had to share was the disappointment of my news. Glumly we resumed our weary search, meeting many others doing the same. At last we came across a young Canadian priest who directed us to a room opposite to the one he shared with other clerics, saying he thought it only had three occupants so far. We knocked on the door indicated but got no answer; tried the door and found it was locked.

The priest, who seemed concerned for us, said that the locked room had a verandah opening on to the front of the block, and suggested we might get in that way. The verandah door was closed, but through the glass we could see two beds, an armchair and a small amount of luggage, so it seemed there was room for the four of us as well.

"Why not climb over the verandah wall and wait there till the other people return?" the priest suggested.

These were certainly strange days, when one could be aided and abetted by another (and a clergyman at that!) to poach on someone else's preserves — for although no one had any more rights to accommodation than anyone else, possession seemed to be nine points of the law.

We took the priest's advice, and the original occupants of the room — an elderly couple and their married daughter — were astounded when they returned and found four lodgers on the verandah. We explained our predicament and they said we could stay the night with them, as the friends for whom they were keeping spaces were not expected to arrive until the next day. They also told us that camp beds could be obtained from one of the bungalows (formerly prison officers' quarters), so despite our weariness, we tramped off to find the bungalow, which was up quite a steep hill. We were lucky enough to get a heavy teak-framed camp bed apiece, and staggered back to the room with them. We had each brought a blanket from the Queen Mary so now, with a roof and a bed, we felt we could relax until the next morning. There was no sign of any issue of food, so we shared one of our tins of meat as our evening meal.

Although our bodies were tired, our minds were too occupied to allow us much sleep. We were all very hazy as to how we were going to exist here. After our experiences with the Japanese at the Jockey Club, we were apprehensive about our future in their hands. With such a lot to think about, we woke early, and after a sketchy toilet (sketchy because the bathroom had to serve over twenty people) Connie and I set off to resume the hunt for a home.

Everyone seemed anxious and confused, and nothing appeared to be organised. We heard the Japanese had sent some sacks of rice, and a few public-spirited souls with more initiative than the rest had got together and were boiling the rice in wash boilers found in the flats. Around midday, while still weaving in and out of the blocks seeking accommodation, we saw a queue beginning to form in the courtyard between the blocks, so joined it. I took my small Canton china rice bowl as a container in preference to the only other possibility — my looted teapot. In the fullness of time we each received a lump of boiled rice and hurried back to the verandah room to eat it before it got cold.

The long wait in the queue had brought us up to date with the latest rumours, chief among which was that another load of internees was due to arrive that afternoon by sea. I hoped Olive and Barbara would be among them, so the need for accommodation began to be more urgent in my eyes. Our search was still without success when I noticed a general exodus in the direction of where the jetty was said to be: it was just beyond the camp boundary, and so far below us as to be out of our line of vision. I tagged along with the rest until a Japanese sentry barred our way; then we all sat down on the parched grass to wait and watch. Far below, and about half a mile out in the bay, toy-like figures were transferring from a ferry to a junk, which then edged slowly towards the land below us and out of sight. After what seemed an age, people came scrambling up the hill, and what a sorry-looking lot they were. There were touching scenes as husbands and wives were re-united. In many cases, neither had known until now whether the other had survived the battle or not, and there were tears of relief and thankfulness. All clung to their possessions.

Presently I heard a cry of "MUM" in a familiar voice, and there was Barbara stumbling towards me over the uneven ground. She was very pallid and her glasses had broken and been roughly repaired by being tied to the frame of an old pair of sunglasses. She had a rolled-up blanket strapped across her, bandolier fashion, and staggered under a heavy bundle of her precious possessions. But she was all smiles, and no wonder. For the past three weeks she and her group had been confined to brothel-type hotels with insufficient food, no exercise other than pacing the flat roof at set times, and no outlook other than the street below and crowded Chinese tenements opposite. After that, Stanley seemed a positive paradise. We both wept. There was such a change in the trim young lady who used to go daily to the office, and I had not realised that my changed appearance would upset her just as hers upset me.

She told me afterwards that I started to tell her at least ten different tales during the short walk to the flats, but that she didn't hear the ends of any of them for days. She had had no contact with Mabel, but did have news of Olive; while being conducted from the hotel to the seafront that morning to embark, she had seen Olive and her group, waving from the verandah of another Chinese hotel. Barbara had had visits while in her hotel from our amah Ah Ding. The guards on the door had not allowed much exchange of conversation through the door, but the loyal little amah made several trips, each time bringing as many clothes and other articles from our flat as her small rattan basket could carry.

"She didn't dare bring a bigger basket, in case it looked suspicious," Barbara said. "She'd have been shot if the Japanese thought she was looting. And she pulled her hair over her face to look like a country bumpkin so that the enemy wouldn't suspect she was helping Europeans."

I heard later that Ah Ding also tracked Olive down at her hotel and took clothes to her, mainly unworn silk underwear — hardly suitable for camp wear, but invaluable to sell when we desperately needed money.

★ ★ ★

Back in the room, a difficult situation had arisen. The family's friends had also arrived on the ferry and it was absolutely essential that the rest of us find alternative accommodation. It was nearing 5 o'clock when our second (and last) meal was due, and the queue was already forming. By the time we had lined up with hundreds of others and eaten the rice, darkness was gathering.

"You'd better spend tonight here with us," our hosts said. "We can all squeeze in somehow."

No more beds were available, so two people slept on the little verandah, one on a steel hospital stretcher, the other rolled up in a blanket, and Barbara joined me on the camp bed until it gave an ominous crack, when she curled up in the wicker chair.

Early next morning, Connie, Barbara and I had a meagre breakfast from our little stocks, then set off separately to find a home. Most of yesterday's arrivals were doing the same, as many like ourselves had only found temporary shelter for the night. As the day wore on without success, we feared we would after all have to resign ourselves to settling in one of the draughty hallways. Many had already done so, and very forlorn they looked. Then Connie dashed up to me and fairly ran me along the corridor and upstairs to the first floor, explaining she had found a room with only one occupant, another ANS. We did not know her, but she welcomed us in; apparently four other people had shared the room with her the previous night but had just left to join friends in other rooms. We lost no time in moving in ourselves and our belongings before any others could stake their claims on the place, where we could remain — at least until the Japanese thought up something else for us.

Our "castle" was the back bedroom, measuring about 12 feet square, of a four-roomed flat overlooking the grassed courtyard where in happier times the family laundry had fluttered. There was a spare camp bed which Barbara took over, a small chest of drawers, a small glass-fronted bookcase and a wooden chair, which had survived from the original flat furniture, also a large wooden dolls' house; in all this we were very fortunate as most rooms had nothing. We chose positions for our beds, allotted a drawer and shelf to each of us in the much prized furniture, and so began our long tenancy of Room 19, Block 3, Married Quarters, Stanley Civilian Internment Camp. (The name "Married Quarters" had no connection with the present occupants — it just happened that these particular flats had been allotted to married British prison officers and their families before the war.) To my great relief, Olive turned up safe and sound in camp the next day with the Food Control unit; how thankful I was that our accommodation problem was solved by then, as we had been able to keep a space for her.

Several bungalows, the former quarters of Indian prison staff, and an ex-boarding school (St Stephen's) within the camp precincts were also used for our accommodation. St Stephen's also contained a large hall which became the camp school in the daytime, and the venue for entertainment in the evenings as well as church services on Sundays. Among a group of later arrivals was someone who had recently seen Mabel at the Military Hospital.

"She's very well, and doing a grand job of work," my informant assured me.

It seemed hardly possible that the girls and I had found each other again after all the chaotic and terrifying days so recently passed. Now, whatever hardships lay ahead of us, I felt we had survived the worst. After the first days of confusion when no one seemed to be in charge, it was marvellous how quickly things became organised, and we settled down to a life which bore no relation to our previous existence.

★ ★ ★

A Japanese commandant was in charge of the camp and lived in an ex-prison officer's staff bungalow on a rise

140

above our quarters. He ruled through the Representative of Internees (our Colonial Secretary) and an elected camp council. Each block of flats elected its own representative — inevitably known as the "Block Head". Every morning the correct number of internees in each block had to be accounted for by the Japanese before movement about the camp was allowed.

On Friday mornings, we all had to assemble in ranks outside our respective blocks and await the arrival of Japanese officials to count us. The whole operation took some time as the party not only had to count those on parade, but also had to tour the blocks to count internees who were certified too ill to leave their rooms. After some weeks, the Japanese tired of all the stair-climbing involved to count the sick, and decreed that in future all sick people must present themselves at their windows and be counted from there.

One day a new order was given: when the inspection party was passing, we must all bow from the waist. This caused so much hilarity — no two people bowing at the same second or at the same angle, and everyone watching everyone else out of the corner of an eye in an attempt to synchronise, that it was soon abandoned.

At first, our food queues were watched over by a few Japanese sentries armed with tommy guns, but after a time they apparently realised we were not likely to riot or stampede, so gave up the practice.

★　★　★

Winston's three months soon passed, and now new estimates of the length of our incarceration were being made. You could see them pencilled on walls, and hear every variety of forecast.

How often you must have heard the remark: "If I had my time over again, I'd like to be a . . ." Well, in Stanley, you could volunteer for whatever job you fancied! There was no shortage of volunteers for the food kitchens, as workers there received double rations when on duty; in fact, most jobs carried a degree of extra food according to the amount of hard labour involved.

The medical and teaching professions carried on their good work in camp, but you would find the Colony's bank managers, shipping executives and civil servants chopping up the logs supplied for the kitchen fires; sweeping the drains and gutters; tending the vegetable gardens; mending fuses; staffing the camp workshop and turning out whatever was requested, from a soup ladle to a surgical instrument — from the crudest of materials; wheeling patients to and from the hospital on stretchers, and grave-digging. The women, mainly formerly housewives with amahs to do all the work in the home, and others used only to office work, became vegetable cutters, or helped out at the hospital as assistant nurses and laundrymaids. Those handy with a needle mended and refurbished clothing for others — mainly bachelors and grass-widowers. This last became my chief job in camp, though I also took a turn with the vegetable squad.

142

Very early on, the original idea of one central kitchen to serve the whole camp had to be abandoned as the quarters were well spread out. Instead, handymen adapted garages and outhouses so that each group of buildings had its own communal kitchen. The problem of cooking utensils was solved when someone recalled that there were a number of large iron pans in what had been a wartime outdoor communal rice kitchen in Stanley Village just outside the camp precincts. The Japanese guard at the boundary agreed (when handed a gold watch) to co-operate in allowing one internee to pass out of the camp to collect the pans.

I am afraid the kitchen workers were always suspected of filching food by the rest of us. (One helper was caught returning from kitchen duty with a good-sized fish down the side of his wellington boot.) Most of the cooks were "makee-learns", but the materials supplied for their apprentice hands to work on needed no great expertise. It was just a case of boiling rice, and chopping washing and boiling whatever vegetables were supplied — usually lettuce and water melon, sometimes cucumbers and pak choi (white Chinese cabbage). Now and again there was some meat or fish, but very little of it.

The actual distribution of the cooked food was no easy task. No matter how the kitchen committee schemed and planned, there were always the grumblers. To ensure equal helpings for all, measures were fashioned out of small tins nailed on sticks (usually, a 12 oz round corned beef tin). The kitchen supervisor — his a thankless task if ever there was one — would decide, according to the amount of stew available, whether the ration should be a full tin each, three quarters or half a tin, then the servers had to keep the stew well stirred with a stick to try to ensure that each got a piece of vegetable — or meat, if any.

The rice boiling produced an unexpected bonus — sheets of burnt rice which had to be prised from the sides of the boilers. It was something to scrunch and chew and had a nutty flavour which compensated for the tasteless stew, but it played havoc with dental fillings.

We were served with two meals daily, one at 11 a.m. and supper at 5 p.m. In the Married Quarters blocks, the serving was always done in the central compound. An old door, laid flat on four rough wooden posts, was the serving table. No one now got the chance to come twice in the queue (as had happened sometimes in the early disorganised days) for a checker stood there with a list of his block residents. You received your rice first, ladled from a zinc bath. The ladle had frequently to be dipped in a bowl of hot water to loosen the grains which stuck to it (so lessening the ration). The small quantity of rice grains collected in this bowl became the server's recognised perks. The serving was supervised by a trusted person who could be relied upon to show no favouritism to his friends. The stew looked very unappetising as your share was scooped out of a large bin.

No crockery or cutlery was supplied; consequently, every variety of container was brought to the queue for food collection — odd china plates, saucers, chow bowls, sections of aluminium food carriers, empty tins, enamel measuring jugs, kidney dishes, oblong medical trays, a baby's potty, an attractive plated ice-bucket — even an opal lampshade which the owner used with his thumb stuck through the whole until he could devise a proper plug. I still have the small Canton china bowl I used until it got broken. (I had it rivetted after the war and it now reposes in honourable retirement in my china cabinet.) I also acquired the top of a large vacuum flask which had a handle; a friend reversed the handle and thereafter I used it to collect my rice — it was known in the queue as the Ascot Cup, as it looked so opulent among the other makeshift containers. It now does duty as a pot plant holder.

Difference in containers, yes, but difference in the ration received — never! Anyone who considered his share to be underweight could take it to be weighed by a helper who presided over a small pair of scales. He would make up any deficit — or deduct any excess, this latter possibility discouraging too many complaints!

If there was any food left over after all had been served, it was distributed as "seconds" to each room in rotation, a strict record being kept by the Block Head. You might get seconds once in two or three months, and the possibility added a little zest to life. When the kitchen staff learned to be really clever with the rations and produced "meat balls" (ingredients mainly sweet potato), and "pasties" (chopped up vegetables enclosed in a rice flour crust), the seconds list had to be classified, as there was no comparison between a second helping of melon or lettuce stew and a second meat ball!

The only food which was not rationed was fish soup (said to be beneficial if only you could stomach it), and seeds from pumpkins. The seeds were just about chewable if roasted, but those who actually ate them soon found themselves passing worms, pumpkin seeds apparently being one of the ingredients of medicines for their elimination.

So much for our food. Nothing was supplied to drink except the water in the taps. In our block, the laundry boilers found in the flats were kept on the go all day long, always with patient queues. The hot water in our block was distributed by an indefatigable old man whose zeal for his job made him a monarch. Nothing seemed to give him more satisfaction than to halt the serving when the boiler was half empty, walk down the queue doing some sort of arithmetic, then point to someone near the end and say, "No good you waiting for this lot — it won't reach you." Even if you were lucky enough to be included in the first count, you might well be eliminated on the second or third, as the boiler gradually emptied. No wonder someone had chalked on the wall above the boiler, "Never have so many waited so long for so little".

Barbara came home in tears one day because she had been refused her ration of hot water, the man having heard her say she intended using it to wash her hair. (There was no hot water piped to any of the bathrooms.)

146

In the first months, some people were lucky enough to have little stocks of tea or coffee, but most of us just drank hot water out of old tins until we were given cheap enamel mugs, also plates. Later, a couple of ounces of tea each were supplied every few weeks, but never enough.

Even for Hong Kong, those early weeks of 1942 were cold. We felt it the more because our clothes were few, bedding inadequate, there was no heating of any sort, and our food was insufficient and tasteless. Morale was very low, with so many wives uncertain if their husbands in the fighting forces had survived the war.

Our medical experts caused representations to be made to the Japanese authorities for a more varied and adequate diet, pointing out that our present calorific intake was well below what was universally considered to be the minimum for survival. The Japanese reply was that better food would be supplied if a large sum of money was guaranteed by some responsible body. This was speedily arranged by businessmen connected with the leading Hong Kong firms, and the rations then improved. Fish appeared quite frequently, though sometimes it was decidedly off and would be condemned as unfit for human consumption. It was then buried — but I would not like to say how much of it was later disinterred, cooked and eaten by those who knew of its resting place.

With everyone so hungry, it was important that each had a fair share; not too difficult to arrange with the liquid stew where water could always be added to make up the required quantity, but dividing pieces of fish into the exact number of identical portions was another matter. There was the day when something went wrong with the counting and there was no fish left for a few people at the end of our queue — just the fish stew, which was simply the water the fish had been boiled in. One man refused to be placated by a large helping of the stew with some extra rice to make up.

"I want my piece of fish," he declared. "The Japanese sent in fish for us all, and I want to know where my piece is!"

When the rations included meat, the bones were recovered after stewing and charred, ground to powder, and distributed to us to sprinkle on our food as a form of calcium. It was gritty and unpleasant, but no doubt our systems benefited for the short period that meat was supplied and bones available.

After a while bags of flour appeared in the rations, but so full of weevils that the kitchen staff could not cope with the job of de-weevilling, so the flour was issued uncooked, each individual cleaning up his own share and cooking it according to taste; we were allowed to take our home-made dough (using a yeast culture made from a piece of sweet potato) to the ovens in the kitchen and have them baked. I may mention that the de-weevilling operations did not last long. It was a tedious job, and we found that unless you well and truly squashed each creature as you unearthed it, some of the little blighters would fly back into their cosy home; eventually, most of us decided that as the weevils had been born and bred in the flour, they might as well be cooked in it it too — they were all protein which we needed badly, and did not appear to do us any harm.

A fringe benefit of the flour issue was the acquisition of the empty flour bags which were much prized as material for underwear and shirts. We could all have been well kitted out had the issue not suddenly been discontinued after a few months It was while flour was still being issued that I fell ill and had a hysterectomy and a long stay in hospital. I was keen to get back to our room to convalesce, but the girls kept urging me to stay in hospital as long as I could, as the rations were better cooked in the small hospital unit, and sometimes included certain extras which I would miss out on back in the block. (I must mention here that these extras, while they lasted, came from private supplies from the Sisters' quarters at Queen Mary Hospital which had been brought into the camp and were generously used to supplement the diet of the very sick.) It transpired eventually that there was another reason why they didn't want me home yet. "We use your bed to put the dough to rise all night," she explained. "There was too much draught anywhere else, but in your bed with your big coat on top, it rises beautifully. Some of the others in the flat bring theirs along to us too." When I was finally discharged I was delighted to find that my weight had gone down to 120 pounds — a loss of about 70 pounds; but the girls were most distressed at the new "me", and thereafter Olive especially was always anxious on my behalf. From time to time most of us suffered from enteritis and dysentery as a result of the poor-quality vegetables, and often I just couldn't stomach the greens on my plate in case they caused me more tummy trouble.

"You've got to eat your greens, Mum," Olive said one day when I left them.

"I just can't today," I protested. We argued about for some time, then Olive yelled, "Go on, then, DIE!" and collapsed on the bed in a torrent of tears, belying the harshness of her words.

When it became apparent that no more flour would be forthcoming, the kitchen staff turned its attention to making bread from rice flour ground on large, primitive but most effective stone grinders supplied by the Japanese. Once established, the daily slice of rice bread became something to look forward to as a real luxury, each slice being meticulously measured out by the Block Head.

One great improvement made by our captors was the innovation of a canteen. Each week a selection of what were to us luxury foods — cocoa, coffee, tea, wong tong (coarse brown sugar in bars), peanuts etc. was sent into the camp for sale. The problem then was money.

It was not usual for Europeans in Hong Kong to keep much cash in their homes, as bills were paid monthly by cheque. Consequently, when war broke out the majority of us had very little money in our pockets. Some people managed to get to the banks and drew money before conditions became too impossible, but most of us came into camp with what remained in our purses, plus a few dollars received from our war units for the first two weeks' duty when the pay corps was still functioning.

When the Japanese started a modest scale of payment to service personnel in the military camps, the men there were allowed to make monthly allotments to their relatives in Stanley. Often the allotment was no more than one yen (which would buy one banana), but everyone knew what a sacrifice it must have been for the men to send any money at all, as they were even more poorly fed than we were. The meagre allotment meant much more than the money as it proved to the wife in Stanley that her husband was still alive, and as all allotments had to be personally signed for, the wife's signature assured her husband that she was alive. (At that time no letters were allowed between the camps).

There were many people like the girls and I with very small resources, and we feared that the few with money would buy up everything in the canteen and leave nothing for the rest of us. Good old British organisation took care of that, though, as each person was allowed to spend only a specified amount. The queue for the very first canteen session began to form just after daybreak. Olive joined it at 7 a.m. I relieved her at 11.30 a.m. and Barbara took over at 1.30 p.m.; she returned to the room at 3.30 p.m. with a small packet of curry powder — all that was available when her turn came.

At a later date, we were able to buy rolled oats. For a few glorious weeks we were allowed to cook in the evenings on one of the kitchen's small electric cookers — that is, if you didn't mind another session of queuing for your turn. Some, like us, made porridge; others re-boiled their rice, or fried up little messes in makeshift pans. Anxiously one waited to edge one's tin on the stove, then gradually got it nearer to an actual ring. Everything had to be cooked at high speed so as to take as little time as possible out of consideration for the others waiting, so our porridge was generally half-cooked and lumpy, but never before (or since) has porridge tasted so good — even without milk or sugar.

For some nights it had been noticed that there was always a large white enamel pail with lid boiling away on one of the rings — something to do with the communal kitchen, we assumed. One evening, someone more curious than the rest lifted the lid and discovered the contents to be someone's laundry — hankies, underwear and a sheet with the owner's name on it — one of the kitchen staff. Public opinion was outraged that she should consider herself entitled to the luxury of boiling her clothes and depriving many of us from getting our bit of cooking done; it was indignantly pointed out to her that many internees had waited over an hour to cook their mess of potage, and that this time could well have been halved had her pail not been continually occupying the largest hotplate. She was quite unimpressed by our complaints. "I always like my sheets boiled," she explained airily. She was very lucky to have the luxury of sheets in the plural, but thereafter her pail was removed to the floor whenever it was found on a hotplate.

★ ★ ★

As if our anxieties about survival were not enough, we had two other serious alarms during those first few months. The first came suddenly one cold, wet day when we were all ordered to leave our rooms and assemble on an ex-sports ground near the jetty. Off we trekked, apprehensive and anxious, not knowing whether we were to be massacred, shipped off somewhere, or merely counted. After a long wait, all that happened was that we were very cursorily searched, but during our absence our rooms were thoroughly examined, evidently to see if we had any forbidden possessions such as wireless sets, cameras etc. My main concern when we heard that a search was on was not for any valuables in our room as there were none, but for our last tin of sausages which we had opened the night before and half of which had been saved for another meal. We were overjoyed to find the four sausages still in the tin on our return.

The second scare started as a rumour which no one took seriously; someone reported that one of the Indian camp guards had seen a tiger at night in the vicinity of the camp hospital. Tigers are not indigenous to Hong Kong island and the report was dismissed as a joke — or maybe the guard had had an overdose of Japanese saki.

A few nights later, a woman internee living with twenty others in a small bungalow saw a large animal cross the garden and disappear into thick bushes nearby. She alerted her room-mates but of course everyone thought she had been dreaming. Next day, the Japanese were seen to be searching among the scrub and bushes on the hillsides around the camp, so now the tiger and its possible origins became the topic of the hour.

Conjectures were many: an animal may have escaped from a private zoo kept by a wealthy Chinese, or one might have escaped from a circus which was visiting the Colony at the outbreak of war; it might have swum across the harbour from the mainland (as one had done years ago and mauled some people before it was shot). Most internees, however, were inclined to ridicule the whole thing, but for all that we felt rather nervous at night and kept our room doors closed, for the main doors in the blocks had been removed and put to other uses, so there was free entrance for the tiger or anything else if it chose to pay us a visit.

A trip to the toilet at night meant braving the lightless passage. One of our neighbours had to get up in the night; she reached the bathroom safely and closed the door. Once enthroned, her eyes grew used to the darkness and she saw a large dark mass between the end of the bath and the wall. Cold with fear, she hardly dared breathe, her eyes never leaving the dark figure as she watched for any sign of movement. But there was none, and after a while common sense took over and she realised that any tiger would have pounced immediately, so scuttled back to her room. Next morning she went to investigate the cause of her fright — someone had left an open wet umbrella in the corner to dry off, and that was her tiger!

The rumours were just beginning to lose ground when one morning, the pad marks of a large animal were found on the sandy soil near the hospital. I think everyone in the camp went to view them. Soon after, we were told the Japanese had tracked the tiger down and shot it. A butcher — the manager of the Dairy Farm Company — was in camp with us, and the Japanese took him off to skin the animal. A photograph of the carcase, slung between bamboo poles, appeared in the Japanese newspaper which sometimes was sent into camp. The tiger was massive, and we all marvelled that it could have roamed about for so long without attacking any one, but perhaps skinny, half-starved internees didn't look particularly appetising, even to a hungry tiger.

★ ★ ★

Despite the poor diet, I made a good recovery from my operation and felt so much fitter than I had for months. Olive and Barbara were happy and occupied with their work in the hospital office, and we had all made many new friends. My main anxiety was for Mabel who had not been in good health when the Japanese first attacked, and who was still with the VADs in the Military Hospital. I made repeated pleas to the authorities for her to be sent into camp with us, and one afternoon Barbara almost fell into the room gasping, "Mabel's come!"

It was not long after my operation and I was not able to walk far, but managed the short distance to the outside of the flats, from where I could see my youngest daughter standing on an open lorry, directing the unloading of her luggage — efficient, independent and completely grown up. She had been enjoying life at the hospital, comfortably housed and better fed than we were. She was highly indignant at having been brought into camp prematurely (with several ailing VADs) — especially when she found we had no bed for her and she had to sleep on banked-up suitcases until a young Maryknoll priest gave her his bed when he was repatriated. Within a few weeks of her arrival Mabel had to go into Tweed Bay Hospital for a complete rest; no wonder, for the past five months she had been washing blankets by hand ("And foot," she giggled, having found that trampling them in the bath saved time). She also had to have treatment for a dislocated elbow.

Our small room now housed the three girls and me, a Scotswoman who had moved in when Connie moved out to better accommodation, and Mrs K who had first invited us to join her in the room. We always called her Mrs K because her Hungarian name was too difficult to pronounce; she became one of my dearest friends. Jess, the Scotswoman, had managed to reach camp with an incredible amount of luggage, which included five folding chairs, a large rug and endless boxes and bundles, all of which were somehow wedged into our already crowded room. At the outset she announced to us that she was the world's loudest snorer.

"Just clap your hands and it stops me," she added. When she was not keeping us awake with her nasal arpeggios, she had us teetering on the edge of sleep while she ploughed through *East Lynne* by candlelight. She must have been the only internee with a private supply of candles. It was a relief to us when the

Japanese ordered a total blackout at night — as we had no curtains that meant no lights, so at least Jess could not now set the room on fire. As to the clapping that certainly shut her up for a while, but generally woke up anyone else who had managed to drift off.

Jess could not set foot outside the door without returning with some acquisition, be it food, clothing or soap. It seemed that people were always insisting on giving her things.

"Look what I got in a present!" she would cry as she came home holding up her spoils. The rest of us could walk ourselves footsore, but never met up with any of these generous folk! Yet she too was generous when her sympathies were aroused; when I was ill, she secreted several bowls of the richest soup from the kitchen where she worked.

One day she announced that she had arranged for a male friend to come to our room to chop up our communal cupboard, "because it takes up too much room". Needless to say, the rest of us in Room 19 immediately petitioned our block representative to ban this plan, and the precious cupboard remained intact.

There were so many arguments in the room that Jess was given a room to herself — a tiny ex-boiler room where she could snore to her heart's content.

★ ★ ★

When the girls and I had exhausted our small amount of money in the canteen, we managed to sell some of Olive's silken underwear (which our amah had taken to her in the Chinese hotel) to better-off internees, but the time came when we were completely broke. By now highly desirable food items were on sale, especially powdered egg yolk and duck eggs. We were saved when the Japanese started to send in cigarettes for sale. Every adult was allowed to buy a certain number of packets each time a delivery was made to the camp. Though of the lowest grade Chinese variety, the cigarettes became one of the biggest morale boosters.

"Cigarettes in!" would come the glad cry round the blocks as soon as supplies were seen arriving on the lorry. The girls and I were non-smokers, but we had four neighbours on heavy manual labour who regularly bought our rations from us, offering us a little over the selling price which left us with some money to buy extra food. I had no scruples in doing this little bit of black marketing: it was our only way of getting any money, and there were always plenty of applicants for our share of cigarettes. I could never forget the morning when Mabel fainted from hunger because she was trying to save her slice of bread until the afternoon for a picnic with her friends. We were all most upset about it. Barbara wrote:

> Give us this day our daily bread
> And take from us our daily dread
> That we and ours may not be fed,
> Nor stagger weakly to the bed
> And faint, because of lack of bread.

158

Our constant anxiety about food made all the more shocking my later dreadful lapse over the sale of our life line. A friend called in one day when I was alone in the room and asked if I would be interested in swapping ten packets of cigarettes for a brand new dress.

"What?" I laughed. "Sacrifice precious cigarettes for a dress I'm never likely to wear in camp?"

"You could keep it for when we get out of here," the caller urged. "It's a beautiful dress. It belongs to Sister Callon at the hospital. She asked me to try to get some cigarettes for it, she's had a long spell of night duty and is desperate for a smoke."

Having been a patient in Tweed Bay Hospital several times, I knew how hard the Sisters had to work and how dedicated they were in spite of their hardships (their quarters above the hospital were perhaps the most crowded in the camp) and I suppose some of my sympathy must have shown, for my friend said, "Come up to my room and see the dress."

Well, I went, I saw and was conquered. There was no point in trying it on, for it certainly would not fit my then scarecrow figure, but Sister Callon and I were about the same build so I knew it would be all right when times (and I) were normal again. The deal was made: I handed over the cigarettes and hid the dress at the bottom of the suitcase in which we kept the only decent things we had. I decided I would tell the girls about the transaction at some opportune time — at the back of my mind was the wishful thought that the dress might stay unseen until Victory Day when, in the general excitement, my lapse would not seem so serious.

But I felt as though I had committed a crime; here we were on the verge of starvation, and I had squandered the equivalent of 200 yen (which could buy ten eggs) on finery I might not even live to wear. The more I reflected on it, the worse my folly seemed. Luckily, cigarette issues were frequent during the following weeks, and I was able to work up a stockpile to replace those I had parted with, so the girls never guessed that for a short time our stocks had been completely depleted.

Discovery came another way. Olive rushed in one day and dragged out the suitcase from under the bed, saying that someone was interested in buying a silk petticoat. Taking out the clothes, she spotted the flat parcel beneath.

"Why, what's this?" she asked.

"Just something of mine," I said, playing for time.

"But whatever is it, wrapped up so carefully? Can I look at it?"

There was nothing I could think of to say to stop her, so she folded back the wrappings; her exclamations of admiration of the dress ended with just what I dreaded: "Wherever did you get it from?"

"Oh, in a swap," I tried to speak casually.

"What on earth did you have to swap for a lovely thing like that?" went on my inquisitor.

"Just some cigarettes."

"Cigarettes?" she repeated incredulously. "For a dress? Oh Mum, whatever were you thinking about?"

Then came the inevitable question: "How many packets?"

For a moment, I recalled the many times when the girls were small and I was on the other end of such cross-examinations. It did not seem all that long ago, and now the position was reversed and here I stood wilting under the accusing and distressed eyes of my eldest daughter. I launched into the whole story. She heard me out, then pronounced in her blunt way, "Well, after that, you almost deserve to starve! Why on earth couldn't you have given Miss Callon a packet as a present, instead of parting with TEN, when you knew we wanted the cigarette money for the canteen?"

She was perfectly justified in her anger, for she had frequently made sacrifices for me when I was ill, giving me her meagre sugar ration and willingly sharing money from the sale of her clothes between us all. I felt terrible about it, and an utter fool.

When the other two girls came they had to hear all about the business, then the dress was put away and never mentioned again in camp. After our release, I was able to wear it, but I can't say I got much pleasure from it: as sure as anyone admired it, they were always informed by one of the girls of its history. I'm sure Miss Callon got more satisfaction from her side of the swap than I did!

★　★　★

Some of the more desperate smokers made their own cigarettes when there was a long gap between issues.

Butts were carefully saved and re-rolled. Only the very affluent discarded them, and there were plenty of scavengers on the lookout for them. Dried pine-needles, leaves of various kinds (even used tea leaves) all made acceptable blends. It was quite amusing, although pathetic, to hear some men exchanging tobacco recipes just as women do cookery recipes. The care and concentration lavished on the preparation of the ingredients for the various blends was worthy of a scientist intent on his latest experiment.

The pipe smokers were sometimes able to buy evil-smelling "suk yin" (Chinese tobacco), and blended this with their own home-made mixture; to non-smokers, the resultant aroma beggars description.

With the occasional cigarette money we were able to shop at the canteen again, and also, by devious means, bought a tiny electric hotplate. From time to time the Japanese allowed a van load of camp patients to be taken into the French Hospital in town for x-ray, as there was no such equipment in Tweed Bay Hospital. I think nearly every patient for x-ray went off with a shopping list as long as his arm. He himself could not do the shopping as the internee patients were not allowed out of the hospital; but there were a number of workers in the hospital who did the shopping for them. Luckily our hot-plate arrived before the Japanese found out about the covert shopping expeditions and suspended the x-ray scheme for a time. The hot-plate was invaluable for scorching up rice and giving it a different taste, our pan an empty herring tin, wiped round with a piece of rag dipped in the precious peanut oil ration — one dessertspoonful each once every ten days or so. Before long the hot plates began to suffer from excessive use, and the elements were continually breaking so you sat on the floor beside the hotplate with a pair of scissors and some thin strips of tin and did any running repairs needed between cooking. Sometimes you might have three or four breakdowns in one cooking session.

Ultimately the electricity load became too heavy with so many hotplates on the go, and they were banned. Now we fell back on a favoured Chinese method — chatty cooking. A chatty was a deep earthenware container for the food beneath which was a shelf on which you burned (in normal times) pieces of charcoal, but lacking that commodity in camp, fir cones and twigs. Some people made their own chatties out of large tins, but in our room we were lucky in having a small fireplace which was easily converted into a built-in chatty with the aid of a few old bricks. Our neighbours came to use it too, providing their own fuel of course. The great advantage of the chatty was that it required very little fuel, which was just as well, as it took ages to collect the only sort available in the camp — fir cones and twigs. (The wooden dolls' house which was in the flat when we took up residence had long since been used for firewood.)

Weird and wonderful dishes were contrived and concocted by trial and error on that chatty. Fried sweet potato leaves, carrot tops, banana skins, were the ingredients of one internee's fry-up. Pancakes were made of rice flour and water, "puddings" by mixing rice

163

flour into a dough, adding chopped carrot tops and a little yeast, then enclosing the result lump in a tin with a lid and burying the tin in the embers of the fire: the result was edible — but only just!

★ ★ ★

With the coming of warm weather, the canteen and better rations, morale rapidly improved. It received yet another boost — a rumour started that each of us would receive a food parcel of our own selection to the value of HK$75! We didn't really believe it, but all the same it was a good talking point. Next we were told to make out our individual lists; still feeling the whole thing must be a farce, we nevertheless carefully compiled our orders just in case the age of miracles had not yet passed. There many people who maintained it was a waste of time to make this list, but I never heard of anyone carrying this conviction so far as to abstain from submitting his.

Excitement was fever high when, some weeks later, a few of the parcels arrived, just as ordered. It was agonising waiting for the next batch, hoping yours would be among them. There was also the ever-present anxiety that the Japanese might have a change of heart and scrap the whole scheme. But eventually we did all receive our parcels, and for a while the quarters reeked with the delectable smell of bacon frying and coffee brewing, and other lovely cooking smells almost forgotten.

Most people ordered nothing but food, but some included a few simple medicines, toilet articles or sewing aids. I included a bottle of Owbridges Lung Tonic as a standby against coughs. Alas, it was not allowed to be a standby for long; one hungry day Mabel eyed it, and with the argument that it might go bad in the hot weather if we kept it any longer, she talked me into agreeing to it being used as a spread on our rice bread, and it was absolutely delicious.

One woman's parcel incredibly consisted entirely of cosmetics. The most sensible was the man who ordered a couple of live chickens. Although hard put to it to keep them fed, he had his reward of the occasional egg, and ultimately a few tasty meals. It was a pity no one thought of asking for a pair of rabbits, as they would have solved our meat problem.

★　★　★

With our little stock of luxuries from the parcels, and the regular weekly canteens, life really became worth living again after the initial months of cold, misery and hunger, especially when, after months without communication with the outside world, suddenly one day postcards were distributed to each of us to write to a relative or friend in one of the military camps in Kowloon — a five-word message only. Everyone worked hard to concoct a message which would give maximum information, and in due course the cards were collected by the Japanese for delivery.

165

Some days later a friend of mine was summoned to Japanese Headquarters — "up the hill" in camp slang. There were two possibilities for such a summons — either someone had sent you a food parcel from town, or else you had transgressed camp rules and were in for trouble. Since my friend knew no one in town likely to send her a parcel, she feared she must have unwittingly done something to offend the Japanese, and was very nervous when she presented herself to the Japanese officers.

"Your name Richards?"

She bowed and said it was.

"You write postcard to Corporal Blake?"

Again she agreed.

"What thing you mean on postcard: 'Roll on apple pie days'?"

She explained that Corporal Blake often came to her house before the war and she usually gave him apple pie when he did as it was his favourite pudding, so she simply wanted to remind him of the good times.

Then came an avalanche of questions.

"You think apple pie days come soon?"

"When you think they come?" etc. etc.

By the time she was released she was a wreck after the effort of trying to think up acceptable answers to the endless questions on the same theme.

The cards ultimately reached their destinations, and quite a number of replies came back to us, but there was no word from any of my girls' men friends. We did not know then that all three had been shipped to Japan, Sidney and Arthur on the *Lisbon Maru* which was torpedoed by the Allies; incredibly, both survived, although some 700 did not.

Later we were allowed to send and receive cable-like messages on Red Cross forms to relatives and friends in Britain and other countries, but partly because of world war conditions they certainly didn't travel at cable-like speed! A pencilled message I wrote to my sister in Kent on a Red Cross form on 15th July 1942 was back in my hands in camp with my sister's reply on the back dated 25th February 1943. It didn't matter how old a message was when it arrived: it was treasured as a tangible fragment of Home, family and a world beyond Stanley which brought warmth to heart and soul.

I once had a card from Will's brother in the United States ending, "Can we send you something?"

"Can he just!" groaned Olive. "I can't think of a single thing he could send that we couldn't find a use for — even a packet of pins!"

She was right. There was a pathetic shortage of just about everything. Scissors had to be borrowed from their fortunate owners for hair-cutting, needles for mending clothes. The occasional issues of toilet paper took the form of a coarse fawn product more suited to packing parcels; consequently the fly leaves of most books (and sometimes the other pages too) were removed to fill the need, while any one with spare yen bought the Japanese newspaper which was periodically hawked round the camp, bought not so much for its news value (all the items extolling the new plan for prosperity in South East Asia and fantastic successes of Japanese troops everywhere) but for use as toilet paper.

167

As for clothes, making do became the order of the day. Most men wore shorts which drooped on their spare figures. Shirts, or the remains of them — were worn in winter, but in summer bare chests were the norm.

Many women converted worn dresses and skirts into shorts to wear with blouses. When the latter split through wear and endless washing, they were cut down to become sun tops. Underwear had to be continually mended, as at no time were pants, bras or socks or stockings supplied. One year the Red Cross sent a cargo of brightly coloured T-shirts which delighted us as a change from our faded rags. They also sent khaki shorts of a very peculiar shape; males and females alike wore them if their figures permitted — they were better than our worn-out clothes.

Mabel spent hours unravelling children's outgrown woollies and re-knitting them in some other form, and sewed her fingers raw fashioning shoes for toddlers out of anything stiff that came to hand — even felt trilby hats, a supply of which was, astonishingly, sent into camp. Olive collected enough reeds and long grasses to weave herself a fetching sun hat with brim.

A lot of people went barefoot during the warm weather, trying to save their precious shoes for the winter, not knowing how many winters they would have to last. Now and again a few pairs of black lace-up shoes were sent into camp, but there was always a long waiting list for them, and to qualify for a pair not only had you to prove that your only shoes were worn out, but also you had to have the right size foot for the shoes available.

There were, however, some internees who had been able to bring in good stocks of clothes and always looked well dressed. One very old lady always appeared in the food queue wearing her blue felt hat with a long feather in it. Even when ill and taken to hospital on a stretcher, the hat was still perched on her head. Another had a stock of capes in pastel shades; also silk stockings which gradually became a mass of ladders, but she wore them until she could no longer muster a pair she could get her feet inside.

★ ★ ★

Something mysterious was going on in the camp! More and more people were seen to be using butter and white sugar and other luxuries. The girls and I were not among these lucky people, and the secret did not leak out until the Japanese magnanimously decided to open up an emergency food store, one of many dotted throughout the colony by the Food Control Department to help in case of prolonged siege. This particular store was just outside the camp precincts and someone in the camp had a key to it.

When the Japanese went there to distribute the contents to us, they found a well beaten track from the barbed wire to the store door, and the chaos of a much depleted store within. An immediate search of the whole camp was ordered. The culprits had very little time in which to hide their booty. Some was hastily buried in garden plots. Others secreted tins at the backs of boilers under the large rice pans (thereby causing a few explosions when the boilers were lit and some of the better hidden tins were fired.) In one all-male block, where every single man had been visiting the store night after night, there was scarcely a toilet which could be flushed as the cisterns were choc-a-bloc with tins of bully and butter.

Some police acquaintances of ours had about thirty pounds of loose sugar in their room at the time of the search. They dared not run the risk of being found with it, and decided the only way to dispose of it was to flush it down the lavatory, yet were very loath to part with it. Since they lived on the very top floor there was a faint chance that the searchers might tire of all the stair-climbing and leave them out, so they mapped out a plan to meet the occasion.

One man stationed himself on the verandah where he was able to watch the soldiers' progress as they moved from block to block If they approached the main entrance of his block, he was to whistle a certain tune — a signal to the other three to take up action stations in the lavatory: one ready to empty the sugar down the pan, the second to pull the chain, and the third to seat himself to hide the evidence. If the soldiers actually began to ascend the last flight of stairs to the top floor, the lookout was to whistle a second tune for the deed to be done. They were fortunate: the search party wearied and left out the top floor, so the sugar was reprieved, but no longer was the store a happy hunting ground for venturesome spirits.

170

★ ★ ★

There had always been rumours of repatriation. Sometimes it was even mentioned in official notices, but I don't think we ever thought of it as anything more than a pipe dream until June 1942 when it actually came to pass for the 200 American nationals in the camp. We inherited priceless treasures such as tin openers, crockery, needles etc., and the block they had occupied helped to ease the congestion in the more overcrowded rooms.

Two of the American Maryknoll priests, Fathers Meyer and Hessler, elected to remain in camp to look after their flock — some 400 Catholics. The only other Catholic priest remaining was a young Canadian, Father Murphy, who was in poor health. Enviously we watched the Americans walk off to the jetty to be ferried out to the *Asama Maru* which lay out in the bay — fortified by the hope that it would be our turn next — and soon.

Our dream of early repatriation suffered a severe blow when a team of our strongest men were sent by the Japanese to the jetty to unload six-months' supply of logs for firewood for the communal kitchens.As the year wore on, more long-term projects were undertaken. Rehearsals began for nativity plays among several denominations. A supply of shapeless, sleeveless khaki jerkins were sent and distributed to us (surely unnecessary if we were to be repatriated soon?). But most of all, one saw hints of a weary future in the gradual development of camp gardens. A handful of

171

enthusiastic gardeners had had to withstand much derision at their attempts to grow vegetables in the sandy soil around the blocks and on the hillsides.

"What's the good of taking all that trouble to grow things we won't be here to eat?" jeered the optimists, as the gardeners made countless journeys to collect water for the gardens.

Now, in spite of the hopes of repatriation, things were taking a different turn. A pre-war football pitch within the camp, known to have been laid with good black soil, was marked off into tiny allotments about the size of a hearthrug for which lots were drawn. Unsuccessful applicants had to make do with the unrewarding hillside patches between rocks. The girls and I drew a plot between us. Seeds were sold, not by the packet, but by the measureful, the measure being the screwtop of a small pill bottle. However, much of the garden produce originated in the rations: pieces of sweet potato were sown, and seeds from tomatoes did well, the greenery of the potatoes being cooked and eaten as well as the vegetables themselves. It even proved possible to grow good tomatoes from seeds taken from tinned tomatoes.

When marrows were sent in with the rations, some people sowed a few of the seeds; the plants grew well and wandered all over the other crops, producing plenty of flowers but no marrows. One gardener reported having fried the flowers and declared they tasted like fried eggs! I hurriedly gathered our marrow flowers and fried them, but either I had forgotten how a fried egg tasted, or else the person who made the discovery had!

We spent a little of our cigarette profit on buying a few peanuts from the canteen, germinated each nut in a small tin of soil, then transferred them to the plot. Peanut growing was quite new to us, we could hardly wait the four months necessary for the nuts we hoped had formed in the ground to mature. We couldn't resist occasionally having a little scratch at the soil to see if any had appeared. They had, but two weeks before the estimated date of maturity had been reached, a Japanese order was made that all the ex-football pitch plots were to be turned into communal gardens, and worked by a regular gardening squad to supply the camp kitchens. We were allowed to gather our standing crops on hand-over day. Our peanuts — a surprisingly large quantity — proved to have a slightly earthy taste, and the shells were not as tough as they should have been, but we were very proud of our produce and ate the lot. They were a costly commodity when on sale in the canteen; most people bought them to grind in the rice grinders which turned them into a gritty peanut butter — delicious spread on rice bread.

One internee who had lived in Stanley in pre-war days had owned a hive of bees which he continued to maintain now on the hillside, using his precious sugar ration to keep it going. I don't know how much honey he got in return, but he certainly never had to complain about losing any. Even the Japanese guards respected those bees, although some of them (and a handful of mean internees) had few scruples where the garden crops were concerned.

★ ★ ★

As time went by, it became increasingly difficult to collect fuel for home cooking. Every one was competing for twigs and fir cones — anything burnable. It was really pathetic to watch an elderly man, well in his seventies, sitting patiently making up little bundles of dried grass to burn under his home-made chatty. The Japanese forbade the cutting of branches or trees, but some people took the risk of being caught by the guards and helped themselves when they could get away with it.

Someone in the European-type flats (like ours) suddenly realised the potential supply of firewood at our very feet: The floors were laid with teak parquet squares, each made up of narrow lengths and backed with a tarry substance and easily prised up. You started judiciously by removing the boards beneath the beds, then gradually encroached on the centre island which grew smaller and smaller until at length you went the whole hog and removed the lot. Used sparingly, they provided firewood for ages, and no one minded that the floors thereafter were rough and black instead of smooth and teak-coloured, although walking barefoot wasn't very comfortable.

There was a vast area of this flooring in the former prisoner officers' club, now used as a junior school, church and entertainment hall. This floor was eyed

174

longingly by those who lived in quarters with concrete floors and therefore had no private supply of firewood. Gradually small gaps began to appear at the corners, then one night all the other floorboards disappeared, obviously the work of a fast-moving combine. As with any desirable commodity, there was soon a black market in floorboards, which changed hands at a dozen little slats for a sterling cheque for £10 (redeemable after the war).

* * *

Towards the end of our first year, news reached the camp of the sinking of a ship — the *Lisbon Maru* — en route to Japan with British prisoners of war from Hong Kong. The extent of the loss of life was not known, neither did anyone in Stanley know for certain if their husbands or sons had been on board, so there was much anxiety in the camp. (In fact the boyfriends of both Barbara and Mabel had been on the ship, but were rescued — we knew nothing of this until after the war.)

Just in time to boost morale came authentication of the Red Cross parcel rumours which had been circulating for months. A party of internees were taken into town to help unload the cargo of parcels from the ship on to a junk which was to bring them to the camp. When the loading party returned, they gave glowing reports of the large number of individual parcels, and of bales of bulk foods, but a week passed and no more was heard of a handout; the pessimists began to wonder if the Japanese had changed their minds about giving us the food.

But at last, one wonderful day, the goodies were distributed. We each received a beautiful brown carton whose contents exceeded our wildest dreams: condensed milk, powdered milk, tinned meat, butter and paste; fruit pudding, tea, and a few wrapped sweets which had evaporated as only the papers were left. It would have repaid anyone who has ever helped the Red Cross if they could have seen our happy faces as we gloated over the parcels. No child ever opened its Christmas stocking with more joy.

As well as a parcel, over the next few months we each received a share of the bulk food supplies sent — sugar, dried fruits and tinned meats. The dried fruits were very mildewed, having apparently been a very long time in transit. I used to scrub each prune and pear with an old toothbrush, then dry them in the sun before stewing them.

Well fed for the first time since our war began (Mabel ate her tin of condensed milk by the spoonful the day she opened her parcel), there was for a while an air of well-being throughout the camp; many people began to regain their lost pounds in weight, but no one got anywhere near their pre-war girth, and when our stockpile of extras was exhausted the pounds fell off again.

The long fast between the 5p.m. meal and the next one at 11 the next morning was very trying, especially for those who did not sleep well, so a scheme to provide breakfast was devised. We each sacrificed two ounces of our daily rice ration which the kitchen staff boiled to the consistency of porridge and brought round to the rooms in big zinc baths at eight each morning. It looked like bill sticker's paste, it had neither milk nor sugar, but it was piping hot and it filled the void, thanks to the kitchen staff who had to get up two hours earlier to make it.

★　★　★

By December that year, even the most optimistic were resigned to spending Christmas in camp, and plans made to celebrate as best we could. Carol-singing, nativity plays and concerts were arranged for Christmas week, and for some time beforehand a small portion of food was kept back each day so that the kitchen staff could produce bumper meals on Christmas Day.

On Christmas Eve the plans had to be changed; a woman internee was found to have diphtheria and all indoor gatherings cancelled to try to lessen the chance of an epidemic — a precaution that worked, as no further cases occurred in our camp (although the military camps in Kowloon lost many men from the same disease). Happily the edict did not affect the carol-singing as this was out in the open air; a choir toured the camp, singing outside each block in turn, and also outside the hospital where a baby was born that day. Hearing the well-loved melodies and familiar words, nostalgia and hope filled our hearts.

Christmas Day church services had to be held outdoors. It was a crisp, sunny morning. We R.C.s attended Mass in a large natural grotto among the rocks between the hospital and the (so-called) American Blocks. Next to the makeshift altar, formed by a slab of concrete jammed into a shelf of natural rock, was a small manger (an old market vegetable basket) complete with a borrowed doll — all just as we were used to seeing in our churches in past years. Many were moved to tears at the familiar scene, remembering too the previous Christmas Day when Stanley had been a bitter battleground and loved ones had perished in the carnage.

Presents were camp-made, but doubly precious for that. Olive made me a tiny box made from old cardboard covered with a piece of cloth and embroidered. Barbara gave me an original poem recalling in verse a childhood family Christmas in England, Mabel's contribution being the accompanying illustrations done with borrowed crayons. Both presents are still two of my most cherished possessions.

The entertainments had to be held over until the New Year, and despite the meagre props available, transported us far beyond the confines of the camp. Father Murphy produced the Catholic nativity play; Olive took the part of the Virgin Mary and wore a blue cloak which was really the full skirt of someone's long dress, cleverly arranged with the waistband round her long fair hair, the bodice tucked inside the voluminous skirt draped round her. The manger and Babe were in use again, and in attendance a choir of angels who looked very remote from the lusty little band of youngsters who roamed the camp all day long.

Another attraction was a rich male choir of mixed nationalities which rendered *Holy Night* in Russian, German and English, thus symbolising the unification of Christians all over the world.

After the diphtheria scare was over and the necessity for outdoor church services and meetings ceased, the little grotto became the permanent site of Catholic gatherings and evening services. This gave our congregation far more scope, as heretofore the two communal halls available for church services had to be shared between all denominations, as well as being used for schools every day and concerts in the evenings.

Father Bernard Meyer was a dynamic force in all aspects of camp life. With the aid of a gang of police from his flock, he cemented a permanent altar into the hillside in the grotto, above which the shape of a cross was chiselled in the rock. Small anti-blast hollow blocks, originally used to protect entrances to buildings in the area, were lugged into the grotto and arranged in rows as seats and/or kneelers. Some of us eased the hardness on our bony frames by bringing our own tiny cushions made from scraps of material stuffed with grass; we also always took these with us to concerts, as again there were no seats.

Never have I met any one as practical as Father Meyer. Of farming stock, he had come to China in 1918 when the Maryknoll Mission was first established. Over the years in the mission field, he had absorbed much of the methods of cultivation of native products; now in camp we reaped the benefit of his knowledge when we planted our tiny garden plots.

From the altar on Sundays he delivered practical advice as well as a sermon. When the rations hit a new low, he said "Now, to get the best out of your food, you should lie down and rest for a while after each meal; if you can't lie down for some reason, then sit down." He advised on the best nutritional buys from the canteen as often as he advised on personal problems.

He was an excellent linguist, and at one time held daily classes teaching Mandarin to a group of young American priests who had the bad luck to stop over in Hong Kong, en route to their allotted missions up-country, the day before the Japanese attacked the Colony. These fine young men, brimming over with good spirits and enthusiasm, ran sports activities for young people until the Japanese took them from the camp into town with a view to allowing them to proceed to their original designations. They stayed in the town for quite a while, during which time I received a note from one of them, Father Moore, saying he had managed to visit Happy Valley cemetery and found Will's grave which was undamaged by warfare, although others nearby had not escaped. Later Father Moore sent the girls and me a small food parcel, and it made us weep to think that he had bothered to do so, and at what self-sacrifice.

Father Meyer's practicality extended to every aspect of camp life. His garden plots flourished under his expert hand, and he was often seen walking round the blocks with a sack of vegetables on his back, playing Father Christmas to the elderly and sick who could not garden for themselves. He urged us to do anything that would ease the burden of camp life for others: baby-sitting for harrassed mothers whose husbands were not in Stanley; repairs to clothing for the unattached men; food queuing for the elderly, etc.

He started a system to help the sick. He and the other remaining Maryknoll priest, Father Donald Hessler sometimes received food parcels from friends in town; most of the contents he sold in camp to the moneyed, and used the cash to buy the best source of protein in the canteen — powdered egg yolk. He kept an up-to-date list of the most needy cases, both those in hospital or recuperating in their rooms, and got a group of us on tap to help implement his scheme. You were allotted a particular patient, given a supply of egg yolk which was to be mixed with ground rice in the proportion specified by Father Meyer (it varied according to the degree of seriousness of the patient's condition), then mixed with water and "fried" (a wipe round an old tin with an oily cloth sufficing) as a pancake, and delivered hot to the patient. This daily service was continued as an extra to the normal rations until the patient improved, or was crowded off the list by more deserving cases.

There must be many ex-internees who owe their survival to this bonus food at a time when their need was dire; also, in no mean degree, surely, to the tangible evidence that some one cared enough to do something for them outside the line of duty.

Father Hessler was gentle and young. Once we persuaded him to tell us about his life in the seminary. He said he had always wanted to work in the foreign mission field, and that when he was appointed to China, it was his "wildest dream come true".

"But, Father," I said, "I'm sure that in your wildest dreams you never expected to find yourself missioning a lot of Britishers?"

"No, indeed," he laughed, "but oh boy, did they need it!"

Yes, we had needed the guidance and help of this saintly, humble man, to make the best of our lives under strange and difficult circumstances. He urged us to strive with our own spiritual development, and also to work with each other in a spirit of neighbourliness, bearing with each other's irritating habits, and excusing faults.

Father Murphy was also young; he had a delightful tenor voice and sang at concerts, introducing us to *An Irish Lullaby* long before we heard Bing Crosby sing it in *Going My Way* after the war. He was in very poor health and, much against his will, was repatriated with the Canadians in 1943.

★ ★ ★

By the time we were into our second year of internment, our priests had ferreted out the 400 or so Catholic internees and got to know them personally. We were gradually and persuasively organised into study groups, action groups, choirs and entertainment groups, most sub-divided so that there was a separate section of each for men, women, young people and children. Weekly meetings of each group were held to discuss various topics of life in general, each member being encouraged to take a turn at leading the discussion. The priests attended as many of these meetings as possible, and our grotto was almost continuously occupied. If it rained, meetings took place in a hallway or verandah, or in someone's room if (as in our case) all the occupants were Catholics and did not mind the invasion. Current camp difficulties and moral issues were closely examined, and efforts made to find a solution. Nothing was too much trouble for these dedicated priests who translated the spiritual into the practical.

After Father Murphy's departure, Father Meyer took over the dramatics for Catholics. Let him hear that you had once sung, danced or entertained in any way and you were at once booked for the next Catholic social. If he decided you were suitable for a part in his latest production, in spite of your protests you generally ended up agreeing to try. Useless to argue you had never been on the stage before. "There has to be a first time for everything," he would smile persuasively over the rims of his glasses. "Maybe this is your golden opportunity." When one of the principals in a passion play fell ill the day of the first performance, Father capably took over the part himself.

When on the prowl for stage props and effects, he was indefatigable. Once, he asked me to make 15 beards for the Jewish elders, producing a sample he had manufactured out of tow well-teased out and attached to a foundation of cloth.

"Try to make them all slightly different in shape and length," he urged.

The resulting beards looked most effective, especially after Father had dyed them various shades with a few permanganate crystals mixed to different strengths. The remains of the dye solution he handed to us; Olive's faded cotton skirt was given a new lease of life coloured khaki, and with the remains of the dye we washed the floor (the boards being still with us then).

Other denominations also organised busy programmes for their flocks. A band of lady missionaries took Sunday school classes for the tinies on the green. It was delightful to watch them and to hear their childish voices singing the well known hymns.

As to entertainment — well, we had to make our own. Quite a number of internees had had experience in amateur theatricals — there were even a few pros; we also had many talented singers and musicians, although instruments were scarce, few artistes having had the forethought to include such items when packing for Stanley! A few pianos left by previous owners in the quarters were in constant use.

At first the Japanese did not interest themselves in our shows, but an open air concert on a hot night caught their attention, so much so that they decided to take some photographs of these happy internees — no doubt for propaganda purposes. All the children were sitting on the grass in front of the performing space, while the rest of us stood around in a huge semi-circle. As soon as the photographer's finger moved to click his camera, the youngsters shot up their hands in a V sign;

again he tried, and this time more and more people showed the sign; some children even sat back on their behinds and splayed their legs in a "V" and again spoilt the picture.

We had to pay the price for our fun; concerts were banned for a while, and when they were re-sanctioned, all scripts had to be submitted to the Japanese beforehand and approved before they could be performed. In addition, two Japanese officers attended all future shows to keep an eye on what we were up to. They were highly suspicious of the play scene in *A Midsummer Night's Dream* — the sight of Wall standing with two fingers parted to indicate the chink convinced them that this was a subtle way of introducing that V sign again. Next morning the producers were summoned up the hill and closely questioned on the subject, and eventually satisfied the interrogators that the chink in the wall was a genuine effect always used in this particular play of Shakespeare's. The producers were then asked if this William Shakespeare was in the camp.

Costumes contributed enormously to the success of these entertainments. With our make-do shabby clothes, it was a real tonic to see someone in a pretty dress, or a man in a suit. Certain prized costumes made regular appearances. The nursing sisters' navy-blue capes with scarlet linings were much in demand. A leopard skin coat did yeoman service to portray a voluptuous divan (generally a couple of wooden forms pushed together) when some exotic scene was set up. A cape of dark blue sharkskin banded with deep brick fur was brought into use whenever a part arose for a fashionably dressed woman. The owners of costumes were always very generous in lending them.

The dancing girls in an ambitious ballet looked spot on in baggy trousers made of ancient and holey mosquito netting, dyed to various pale colours with weak solutions of such things as curry powder, mercurichrone and brilliant green. (How could these last items be spared? Ah, the play's the thing!)

For me, one of the most memorable camp plays was *Peter Pan* which Barbara and a group of other enthusiastists produced with an all-child cast. The finished production was far more convincing than a professional one. No buxom female "principal boy" as Peter, but a slim lass of 13 clad in a simple tunic covered with real leaves, his shadow the remnants of someone's wedding veil. The crocodile brought the house down. Played by a thin lanky girl of 14 enveloped in gunny sacks sewn together in a sort of tapered bolster, with eyes, jaws and teeth outlined in chalk, she slithered across the stage using her elbows as propulsion, while the juvenile audience thundered their applause.

There was also a magician in camp whose act at first included the miraculous production of two pigeons, but before long the said pigeons ceased to perform — the magician had evidently found a better use for them.

Fortunately there was quite a number of books in the camp so there was no shortage of play material. Such classics as *The House Master, Call it a Day* and *A Bill of Divorcement* were presented with the polish of professionals. A pierrot concert party sang such topical jingles as:

> Oh Mrs A lived on the Peak,
> Her manners were most flighty;
> But now, like us, she must confess,
> She only has one nightie.

(Living on the Peak pre-war meant that you were one of the upper crust; digs such as this went down well; truly, camp life was proving to be a great leveller in many ways.)

The value of all these shows lay not only in the finished performances, which transported the audience for a few hours into a very different life from the one we were living, but also in the weeks of preparing that preceded them. The people preparing or adapting the script, the wardrobe mistress and stage manager combing the camp to borrow suitable garments and props, the musical arranger experimenting on the piano for appropriate background music or incidental songs — the latter conditioned by what little music was available, and on the memories of the pianists and their assistants. Last but not least, the cast, learning and rehearsing their parts, all were able to forget for long periods at a time their hunger, anxieties and boredom. As for the children's concerts, their rehearsals were treated as glorious play hours, and their parents were glad to know they were occupied and under supervision.

If one had to select a favourite performer in Stanley, I think most internees would vote for Mrs Betty Drown. Every Sunday evening, she sat down at the piano in the clubroom and played non-stop. No programme was announced: Betty merely played as the fancy took her, and a more varied selection of music it would have been hard to find. I think she must have known every tune ever written, and if anyone could not recall a title when making a request, one had only to hum a bit of it and she would play it. When another piano was moved into the hall a second pianist, Ian Heath, accompanied her. When everyone joined in, singing, you couldn't hear the pianos! The audience completely filled the hall, and the overflow perched on window sills, cluttered up the doorways and then covered the green outside. We all became very nostalgic as well remembered favourite tunes filled the evening with melody, bringing back memories of happier days.

Betty's final item was *There'll always be an England*, which either the Japanese did not know or else did not associate with imperialism, although *God Save the King* was forbidden. We got away with singing *Rule Britannia* and another great favourite, *Eleven more months and ten more days*.

When rumours of repatriation for us all were at their highest (after the departure of the Canadians in 1943 we were under the impression that their ship would decant them at Lourenco Marques for onward transmission, then turn round and come back for us) another song was added to the finale, with a rousing chorus in which we all joined lustily — *We're going to sail away*; but unfortunately we didn't. Yet hopefully we clung to yet another rumour which had it that we would be sent to Goa, and inspired another closing theme — "We're going to go to Goa on repatriation day!". This too was sung with great fervour for ages, until it appeared we were NOT going to Goa — or anywhere else, when it was succeeded by an adaptation of an old song, *Has any one seen our ship — the HMS Peculiar?*. By 1945 when news of the advancing Second Front in Europe was trickling through, we were beginning to accept that release would come through victory rather than repatriation, so sang hopefully "When the carrier plane comes to carry us home . . . some . . . day . . . soon".

All these prophecies seemed quite incapable of fulfilment when we sang them so heartily, but they were wonderful dreams to dream; their originators deserve immeasurable credit for their contribution to camp morale.

There were many times when our spirits needed raising. Everyone was deep in gloom the day the Japanese took several civil servants from the camp to the Gaol. Rumour had it that the Japanese had discovered hidden working radios with which the chosen men were suspected of being involved. A few weeks later a notice from the Japanese appeared on the board: the men had been tried and most found guilty and sentenced to death, which sentence, the notice continued, had already been carried out. All this emphasised our helplessness and isolation from the outside world. I was so thankful that Will had died when he did: had he been alive and interned, I knew without doubt he would have been deeply involved with anything to do with clandestine wireless sets, and would have suffered the same horrific fate as those Stanley victims.

One cold wet day when the meal was more meagre than ever, the girls and I were sitting on our beds, scraping with our spoons the last particles of rice from scratchy enamel plates recently issued. We had no dessert, no fruit, and only water to drink in an enamel mug. Our cupboard was empty. There were no curtains at the windows; all the floorboards had gone and we walked on the knobbly under surface.

Suddenly one of the girls began to giggle. "Mum," she said, "do you think this is the day we've come to our cuttings down?"

We roared, especially when Barbara added, "I bet you didn't expect to come with us, Mum!"

★　★　★

Your accommodation having been governed by the accident of your arrival in camp rather by any devised plan, often two or three married couples and single people, male and female, found themselves sharing a room. Sometimes people of mixed temperaments found it very difficult to live almost head to head, and an appeal would be made to the camp billeting officer for a move. As there were no spare bed spaces, moves could only be made by way of mutually agreed swaps. Apart from the rooms vacated by the repatriated

Americans and Canadians, only when a death occurred was there a vacant space.

Every possible nook and cranny was adapted for use as quarters. The tiny kitchen in our flat was converted into a room for a couple with one small child. Sink and fittings were transferred to an outer porch open to the back verandah, and a right of way through the block. Now, if the bathroom was occupied, you had to wash in full view of any one passing through the flats or out in the central courtyard.

Ablutions were always a problem. No hot water was laid on in the flats, so cold water washes only were available. Hong Kong has always had a water problem, and wartime difficulties only enhanced it. There was a time when the Japanese curtailed the water supply to one day in three, so even the luxury of a cold bath in the summer was denied for the baths had to be used to store water for use during "dry" days. In our particular flat, we were each allowed to draw five measures of water a day from the bath — the measure being a 2 lb treacle tin nailed to a stick. With this ration, one had to keep oneself clean and wash one's utensils which only amounted to a mug, a plate and spoon, and fork if you possessed one. Clothes washing had to wait for the day when the water was on.

The toilets could not be flushed automatically on dry days, so we kept an old kerosene tin beneath the wash bowl in the bathroom, removing the waste pipe so that all used water drained into the tin. Every time the tin was full, one of the men residents was summoned to stand on the lavatory seat and pour the water into the cistern. Quarters without baths had even worse problems. They had to trail down to the beach with whatever containers they could muster, and collect sea water for flushing the toilets. A complaint to the Japanese about these difficulties merely brought forth a suggestion that we should dig trenches outside the blocks to use as latrines. As the water situation worsened, the trenches were dug, but a request for privacy screens was rejected and the trenches were never used.

Tempers could run high where any question of usurpation of communal rights was concerned, as witness the case of a woman who persisted in hanging her laundry to drip dry over the communal sink where all her neighbours washed their dishes. A male neighbour finally lost his temper when garments continually got in his way as he washed up, and he pulled the line down. When the lady found her prized sharkshin suit on the floor and accused the offender, he admitted his guilt and told her to hang her laundry in the quadrangle like everyone else. She said she would hang her washing where she liked. He retorted that he would pull it down every time he found it dangling over the sink. There followed more acrimonious exchanges, culminating in a threat from the man "to knock your block off". The woman took him to the camp tribunal for "using threatening language".

The accused was asked, "Did you on the . . . day of . . . threaten to knock this lady's block off?"

"I did," replied the defendant, "and I'll do it again if she hangs her clothes there again."

The tribunal could only admonish the two to keep the peace.

★　★　★

Communal living under semi-starvation conditions created disputes even among families. During the brief flour ration period, the kitchen staff baked small individual loaves. As no two were ever quite the same size or shape, when four were delivered to our room the girls and I each took it in turn to have first choice. There was a dispute one day about whose turn it was; Olive thought it was hers, Barbara declared it was hers and took the best. There was a fierce argument, then Barbara hurled the disputed bun across the room at Olive's face and accepted second choice, but there were tears all round that a little thing like the size of a bun could bring us to such an emotional state. When the flour supply ceased, our daily ration of bread, made from yeast and ground rice, was about half an inch thick and no more than three inches square. The loaves were delivered to each Block Head, who measured it out, cut it and handed round so many pieces to each room. Where there were two or three members of one family, she would hand the total ration for all in one undivided chunk. A mother and adult daughter living next door to us regularly brought their joint portion to me to cut in halves for them, as they thought I would be fairer. Another room near us accommodated five adults, one of whom was always out on some camp chore at the time the bread was delivered; by her orders, the four others in the room had to postpone the division of the loaf until she was present.

* * *

Parents with young children lived under severe strain where they had to share a room with other internees. Trying to keep the youngsters from annoying the other occupants was especially difficult, as most mothers had relied on amahs in peacetime and so were not used to coping with children for 24 hours a day. There were no biscuits or sweets to reward a child for "being good", and no lights allowed after 9 p.m. so it was difficult to pacify a child waking in the night.

A young couple with baby who had the comparative luxury of a tiny ex-amah's room to themselves had a terrible problem: baby Alan cried night after night and kept everyone in the block awake, as it was too hot to close windows. There were so many complaints about the child's yells that the mother became quite ill with worry, so her doctor asked the hospital for some aspirins to help the child to get into a sleeping pattern. The request was refused because aspirins were in short supply and only prescribed for serious cases. The doctor lived near Alan too. "It's either a few aspirins to settle Alan," he declared, "or 500 — one for everyone in the Married Quarters so they can get a good night's sleep." Alan got his aspirins.

People without families, or whose children were grown up, were not always sympathetic as, had the young mothers obeyed the evacuation order, they and their children could have been safely in Australia. Many groused that the small quantity of special foods which came into the camp for young children could have been used for sick adults; this did not necessarily follow, however, for had the children not been in the camp there was no guarantee that any special supplies would have been sent in at all. Trying to bring up a toddler in the same room as four childless women was, as one young mother sobbed, "like having four mothers-in-law."

Meals for the under-threes were prepared in a small kitchen just below our room, and many a hungry day we blissfully sniffed the appetising smell of their "bread" ration being toasted for them. Here too their precious milk was carefully measured out. If it was spilt by the collector on the way home, it could not be replaced.

The children themselves led a glorious carefree existence. They wore the absolute minimum of clothes, and when their shoes wore out they went barefoot. Their mothers could send them out to play, knowing they could not go beyond the confines of the barbed wire. If they should wander to any of the neighbouring blocks, someone would always bring them back. The only traffic was the ration lorry, and so many were watching for its arrival to unload it that there was no danger to the children. They were invaluable as queue-place holders while their parents were busy with other chores. The highlight of the toddlers' day was when the water hydrant in the road was turned on to wash the rice — this was before water rationing. This operation always left a glorious puddle in which they splashed to their hearts' contents. They were as brown as berries, and many had forgotten about any previous way of life.

"When I grow up," one small girl was heard to remark, "I'm going to have four children; one to grind the rice, one to do the washing, one to go to the canteen, and one to collect the water." Evidently she expected to spend the rest of her life in camp conditions.

They scoured the hillsides for the only fruit growing within the camp precincts — berries they called "barley boos", and hard little guavas. Although bereft of the vitamins needed for their proper growth, evidence of deficiencies were not readily apparent, except in a few spindly-legged teenagers.

School-age children had lessons every morning in the two communal halls. There was a wealth of educational talent in Stanley. In addition to the teachers from the schools, there was also the European staff of the Hong Kong University. Textbooks and stationery were extremely limited; all the classes were taught at the same time in one room, but despite this, and the listlessness and lack of concentration caused by poor diet, quite a number of children sat and passed exams to matriculation standard.

About two hundred children were brought into camp, and some 57 more born there; in spite of the privations, the mortality rate among them was very low. A few mothers had managed to bring prams and cots, and these were passed on as they were outgrown, but there were never enough to go round. Four mothers in our block used to take it in turns to push all four babies around in a much treasured pram.

One Japanese official took a snap of a baby born in Stanley and sent it to the father in a camp in Kowloon. This touch of humanity really surprised us, for in general our captors were terribly casual about communications between camps. We could understand it was not always their fault that the rations were poor — after all, we were on an island and our own planes and ships were trying to prevent supplies from reaching it — but there was no excuse for limiting and holding up mail between two camps only about ten miles apart. It took months for a wife in Stanley to hear of the death of her husband in one of the military camps. There was another woman mourning her husband believed killed during the fighting, who got the news that he was alive and well months afterwards.

★ ★ ★

With everyone eating in their rooms, and no insecticides, livestock soon became a menace — first the cockroaches and then the bugs. Probably the bugs arrived in camp with mattresses from the Chinese hotels which some internees brought in. The creatures really got dug in to the camp during a brief period when the Japanese ordered all unattached men to go into Stanley Gaol every night to sleep, taking their bedding with them. We never knew why.

About this time Barbara's camp bed began to give way. She had to get on to it very gingerly, and hardly dared turn over at night in case it collapsed completely. Without much hope, we applied to our Welfare Committee for a replacement. Very soon after a man died, and his bed was brought to us — a single spring bed, with no mattress, but Barbara was highly delighted to have a really sturdy bed. One night in it was enough, though. She scratched all night, and next morning we found it was full of bugs. We ditched it right away, but had inherited the bugs and they stayed with us for the rest of internment. Some took up residence in the picture rail but the majority found shelter in the thick coils and springs of my bed (which had no mattress) and in the patches on the other camp beds. I used to smoke them out frequently, burning paper shavings used as packing in the Red Cross parcels along the springs.

Bugs and cockroaches were not the only uninvited guests. We often left overnight some washed, uncooked rice on the windowsill to dry, ready for grinding into flour the next day. The windows were always open at that time of the year, and we gradually came to realise that the quantity of rice was diminishing overnight. Mabel woke with a screech one night, declaring that something had run across her face. She was sure it was a rat, so the next night we covered the rice with a towel. This did not deter the visitor — he simply gnawed his way through the towel to get at the rice.

"We must get a cat," said Olive (it was her only towel). "If we each give it a spoonful of cooked rice a day, that will be better than letting a rat steal our rice."

A few domestic cats had been found about the camp at the outset and been adopted by animal lovers, so it was not difficult to book a prospective kitten, and in due course Henry joined our family. He really looked like an animal internee! He was just skin and bone, and didn't look as if he would ever stand up to a mouse, let alone a rat. When he stretched, he looked as though he was cut out of cardboard. "No depth to him," as one friend remarked.

He enjoyed the rice diet and, tail erect, was always first in the congee queue in the morning, miaowing loudly; he kept up his raucous wails until we brought our shares into the room, spooned his ration into his tin lid, and blew on it until it was cool enough for him to eat.

Sometimes I gave him a teaspoonful of the tasteless vegetable stew, but this had to be done on the quiet, as Olive objected to my depriving myself of any food. One evening I saved a piece of rice flour pasty to eat in bed last thing at night. Henry was sitting beside me when I ate it, and I fed him tiny crumbs on the palm of my hand. There were no lights of course, so I didn't think Olive would know what I was doing. Unfortunately Henry was a noisy eater.

"Are you feeding that cat with your pasty?" demanded Olive sternly. I had to admit to having given him just a taste, and was strictured not to give him any more. Poor Olive, I think she suffered more than any of the four of us in camp, for she made herself responsible for us all.

Henry's greatest treat was tinned salmon. While the girls and I were all out of the room one day on different ploys, a neighbour brought along a tin of salmon she had just opened — she was one of the fortunate ones with a friend in Hong Kong who sent her parcels. Apparently she felt a little uneasy about the condition of the salmon, so decided to share it between Henry and another cat in the block. I came home before the girls and my nostrils were immediately assailed by the heavenly smell of salmon. Henry was happily asleep on my bed, reeking of salmon. The neighbour had heard me arrive and came to explain. I thanked her, wishing with all my heart that I had been at home to inspect the possibilities of that salmon before passing it on to Henry. Then Mabel arrived. She stopped in her tracks at the door and sniffed. "What can I smell? It's salmon!"

Told the tale, Mabel shared my feeling. But when Olive and Barbara returned and heard the sad story, they refused to lament. "Thank goodness you weren't home to get at it first, Mum," Olive said. "It must have been a bit off. No one in their right senses would throw out a tin of anything these days unless they had real doubts about it. You could have poisoned yourself."

Mabel glared at Henry, saying "If that cat is still alive tomorrow, I'll never forgive it. Half a tin of salmon inside it, and we only get the smell!"

But Henry was in his usual place at the head of the congee queue next morning.

"Look at him!" said Mabel in disgust. "He wasn't even sick after it."

Another treat came Henry's way later, but he didn't get first "go" this time. The daughter of one of the leading black marketeers was to be married: with both money and contacts to obtain supplies, the wedding feast was the envy of all those not invited. On the wedding night we were all in bed, talking in the dark, when the bridegroom tapped on our door.

"I've brought some chicken bones for Henry," he said. "Don't get up, I'll just put them on the floor by the door."

We chorussed our thanks, but the moment he had gone Mabel sprang out of bed. "Chicken bones for Henry indeed! We'll have them first." She handed them round, and we sat up in bed, nibbling round bones that others had already gnawed. I don't think I could have done such a thing in daylight. Henry had to make do with the bones third hand next day.

Thin though he was, his presence certainly deterred any marauding rats from coming to our room. Occasionally other inmates of the flat would borrow Henry when they had had a visit from a rat. He behaved more like a dog than a cat in his attachment to me. He never went out of doors by himself, for which I was thankful — there was always the chance that some hungry person might capture him for the pot. In fact, an elderly bachelor latched on to me for some weeks, accompanying Henry and I on our evening walks round the blocks; when he said something which made me suspect that his friendliness was because he had designs on Henry rather than me, I quickly terminated the friendship!

★　★　★

Thanks mainly to the glorious situation of the camp and the open air life, the general health of internees was quite good as far as infectious and contagious diseases were concerned. Of course the inadequate diet caused every one's weight to drop dramatically, and there were many severe cases of malnutrition, but we suffered no epidemics apart from dysentery and enteritis in the early days, and there were comparatively few deaths.

A sad loss was that of Vi Evans, one of our most cheerful entertainers on the Stanley stage. After a straightforward operation, she remained cyanosed, a condition which could have been corrected had oxygen been available to restore her but none was and so she died, aged 40. Vi had been such a favourite and lively personality that there were crowds at her funeral. Her husband was in one of the military camps in Kowloon, where he too later died.

The sick were admirably cared for in the camp hospital by the doctors and nursing staff of the various hospitals in the Colony. The Sisters, despite their incredibly cramped accommodation on the top floor of Tweed Bay Hospital, always managed to keep their uniforms spick and span although they, like the rest of us, had to queue for their meals and the canteen, grind their rice and do their laundry. The doctors, in addition to their medical work in the hospital or in clinics in the different blocks, took turns with a police working party at sawing up logs to fire the hospital kitchen, and unloading the ration lorry and delivering the hospital's share. Olive happened to be watching the vegetables being unloaded one day. Dr Kirk, the obstetrician, was handed a large pumpkin as part of the hospital ration: while waiting his turn for its weight to be checked on the scales, he gave the pumpkin an experimental balance in his hand and said "About seven pounds, I think."

"However did you know?" asked Olive when his guess proved correct.

"All same new baby," he replied.

Another time, Dr Barwell happened to be on the fish-cleaning squad. He was expertly removing the bones and looked up and said, "If my father could see me now, he would say I was prostituting my profession!"

Many major operations were carried out by tireless surgeons who had to get along on the same miserable rations as the rest of us. I was sitting on the hospital verandah one day, convalescing after my hysterectomy, when I saw one of the professors who had been operating all that morning come from the food queue with a dollop of rice in a kidney dish with the watery stew slopped over it. He sat down on the grassy bank below the hospital and tucked into the food as though it was the most luxurious of meals. Between mouthfuls, he carried on a laughter-laden conversation with another doctor. He was a big built man (though gaunt now) in his late fifties, and could I am sure have eaten three or four times the amount in his dish. But his skill and boundless enthusiasm for his work never waned, despite frustrating shortages of medical supplies.

For a patient who had had an abdominal operation, he devised a shield from an empty sardine tin into which a glass bottom had been fixed in place of the original tin one. The tin was taped to the patient's tummy so that the incision could be inspected without uncovering it.

Several people could be seen walking about with a sling supporting the ball of the foot and attached above the knee. This was the professor's method of relieving drop foot which sometimes afflicted those suffering from beri beri and caused the sufferer to drag the affected leg. I myself had quite a spell of this.

Mabel had a bad fall as a result of which she had to wear a brace. The accident happened just before sunset while she and Barbara were gardening, our plot being on the edge of a 16-foot drop. She was rushed into hospital and the professor had to work against the failing light, no electricity being on. Suspecting a fractured femur, he sent runners all over the camp to collect anything in the way of broom handles, anything suitable for rigging up an emergency splint. By the time it was dark he had her trussed up in a Heath Robinson version of a Thompson splint, with three charcoal irons as counterweights which answered the immediate purpose admirably. (The Chinese used such irons, filled with glowing charcoal, instead of electric ones.)

Despite repeated requests to the Japanese, it was ten weeks before she was taken into town for x-ray, then it was found she had a cracked rib, a broken wrist bone, fractured heel and displaced vertebrae. By this time she was walking on crutches, but was very one-sided and

204

could not straighten her back. The professor tried to devise ways of straightening her up. The first took the form of stout calico straps worn over the shoulders, with a buckled belt leading down to straps round her thighs, but all this chafed her skin. A plaster cast did not work because the plaster supplied would not set, even though she was laid out in the sun to try to dry it. His next idea was the aluminium brace made from ceiling fans found in the flats, with the back stays reinforced with pieces of wood. This really worked. Mabel was allowed to take it off at night, and hung it on the picture rail where a family of bugs promptly moved in to the holes in the wooden supports and bit her badly, so we had to clean out the holes regularly. Thanks to the professor's untiring efforts and ingenuity, her back gradually improved until it was almost straight. When two years after the end of the war, Mabel was in Kowloon Hospital having just had her first baby, a Sister who had nursed her in Stanley looked in the ward.

"Let me see this miracle baby," she said. "The doctors in camp thought you would never be able to have children after that fall." They were proved wrong twice.

★ ★ ★

Coffins were not provided by the Japanese, and there was no wood available in camp to make them, but the workshop did manage to construct one Haddington type coffin with a removable base which was used throughout internment. The only alternative would have been to bury the dead in old rice sacks.

Neither would do for Paddy O. Irish himself, he had a devoted Chinese wife who chose to share internment with him although she could have remained free in town. When Paddy was found to have an incurable disease, his wife was able to get plenty of extra food for him through the black market, and in food parcels sent into camp by her family connections. But no food could save Paddy and he knew it. His one wish was that he would be buried in a proper coffin, so Paddy's wife set about trying to procure one in advance, for camp funerals usually took place on the day of death.

First she tried to get a coffin from the Japanese on payment of a large amount of yen. This did not work so she let it be known throughout the camp that she would pay well if anyone could supply the wood and make the coffin. In this case, money talked: someone obliged, and Paddy had his wish and was buried in his personal coffin. (Some room in the camp was now minus part of a wardrobe which had been in the room when the inmates took over.) His wife, in pursuance of Chinese custom, placed on the coffin lid all his small personal possessions — his rosary, comb, a box of matches and a packet of cigarettes — so that he could make use of them in heaven: the two latter items were eyed longingly by some of the mourners, who could hardly bear to see such waste.

After the funeral, the outcry started. The luxury of a private coffin became the talk of the camp. The supplier had to appear before a camp tribunal and answer charges that he had "moved or caused to be moved from a built-in cupboard a pair of doors, being communal property; that he had also moved (or caused to be moved) two doors from a wardrobe". Somehow, the culprit was able to convince the tribunal that although his action in using communal property to make the coffin was a breach of camp rules, "he had reason to believe that he had sufficient authority for his action". Accordingly, the accused was "discharged".

How footling and pompous these tribunal cases sound now, yet how important they all seemed at the time, when we were so conscious of our individual rights. All the same, I can't think why any of us should have grudged poor Paddy his coffin, however shady the dealings that obtained it, instead of thanking God that we didn't require it ourselves.

★　★　★

The historical Stanley Cemetery became the resting place of those who were killed in this area during the fighting, and those who did not survive camp life. Originally it had been laid out for the pioneer forces garrisoned in Stanley when the British first landed in 1841. Severe epidemics had caused many deaths, and some of the massive tombstones recorded the names of whole families who had died. Many of the tombstones were now pitted with bulletholes, bearing mute testimony to the fierce battle which had raged here at Christmas 1941.

207

One of the old tombstones bore this thought-provoking verse:

> Stranger, when you pass me by,
> As you are now, so once was I.
> As I am now, so will you be,
> Prepare yourself to follow me.

The cemetery had not been used for decades. Now a number of rough crosses marked the graves of soldiers killed in December 1941, and as the years of internment rolled on, rows of new graves appeared, each marked with a small headstone skilfully fashioned by a patient and talented internee from granite slabs previously used for road marking. In due course the makeshift wooden crosses above the war casualties were also replaced by similar granite headstones.

The view from the cemetery was breathtaking, towering hills opposite, on which stood the fort, and the blue sky beyond stretching as far as the eye could see. There among the tombstones, beneath the shade of the casurina trees, internees came seeking some measure of peace and solitude.

I revisited this cemetery many years after the war, and was pleased to find that, although the whole place had been enlarged and redesigned, the little camp headstones have been retained. Many of those who died in the Kowloon camps were re-interred in Stanley, and the cemetery now extends in terraces down the hillside, and an imposing memorial stands at the entrance. Yet even this enlarged cemetery with its rows of crosses looks small when you have seen the appalling number in the main military cemetery at Sai Wan. One can only gaze at all these pathetic memorials and wonder — was Hong Kong worth all that?

★   ★   ★

Although Japanese military yen became the official currency in the Colony, Hong Kong dollars were still accepted for some time, but the high denominational notes were devalued, a $100 note now being worth $80, and a $50 note only $40. Those internees fortunate enough to have any of these found it more profitable to raffle them rather than spend them at their reduced value. At $1 a chance, the seller could realise at least the full $100, while the winner was well pleased with the note, no matter what its current value.

One bright lad made a lot of money by raffling notes he did not possess; he would sell one dollar chances until he had enough cash to buy a big note at its reduced value, then carry on selling more chances until he had amassed quite a profit for himself — then held the raffle. His trick was discovered when for once he was unable to buy a large note in time for the raffle. Thereafter, all raffles had to be officially approved by our Commissioner of Police, the article to be raffled produced beforehand and the number of chances limited.

As time went on, some far-sighted people in town saw a future in exchanging their surplus military yen for gold and other valuables which would represent capital when the Japanese were defeated and the yen rendered worthless. These people made contact with our Formosan camp guards, who in turn contacted internees known to be black market operators. It was made known that if you had any gold or other valuables to sell, black marketeers would carry the deal through for you. You handed him the article and stated your selling price — and then waited hopefully, sometimes quite a long time, for the black marketeer could not hand over your article (through the barbed wire at night) until his particular guard contact was on duty; then the guard had to make a trip to town and show the article to the prospective buyer to examine. If the buyer's offer was favourable, you accepted; if not your article was returned.

Hundreds of these transactions took place, involving very large sums of money, yet I never heard of anyone either losing goods or failing to be paid the agreed price. Of course the guards and the camp contacts all got a rake-off. We sold Olive's engagement ring, a Parker fountain pen, two watches and a gold brooch.

The black marketeers took great risks. While in general the guards not involved as contacts shut their eyes to the traffic, there were occasions when a dealer ran foul of one of them and was in trouble; the Japanese authorities were officially against black marketing, so were ready to pounce on a transgressor.

★　★　★

There came strong rumours of electrical equipment and plant being shipped out of Hong Kong; of motor car bodies being flattened after engines had been removed, and tramlines torn up — all shipped to Japan. All this pointed to what our incurable optimism convinced us would happen — one day the Japanese would walk out of Hong Kong. This started the traffic in sterling cheques.

People who had amassed yen from the sale of gold and jewellery realised that if the war ended suddenly, they could well be left with a pile of worthless yen, so began selling their excess yen for sterling cheques (or a scrap of paper serving the same purpose) to be honoured after the war. There were plenty of people who had nothing to sell so were glad enough to hand over a cheque for some ready money for food. Then the racketeers got busy. They bought yen in bulk and farmed it out in small quantities to those who only dared to write small cheques, lending at a higher rate of exchange than they themselves had paid.

The barbed wire boundaries became a hive of industry at night, not only with the money and gold transations, but also with food supplies. All barbed wire business was "black" from our captors' point of view, so no prices could be put on paper. Everything had to be done by word of mouth. Those brave enough to take the risks of black marketing did a brisk trade, but one was badly bitten one day when canvassing his wares. Passing through the corridors he quietly mentioned the goods he had available, including on this occasion a great rarity — bacon.

"How much a pound?" asked an elderly lady.

He held up five fingers.

"Oh, I'll have a pound," she decided instantly.

"Right!" he called over his shoulder, passing on. "I'll send it over."

Next morning his son brought over the bacon, saying the father would be over later for the money. The buyer immediately fried two fine rashers, and she and her husband ate them with relish. When the dealer called for the money she handed him five yen.

"What's this for?" he asked.

"For the bacon — you said five yen, didn't you?"

"Five hundred yen, madam," he corrected.

"But you said five, you held up five fingers," she said faintly. "We can't pay you 500, we don't possess that much money."

In this difficult situation, the seller went to the camp tribunal to see if he could somehow recover his loss. It was decided that there had been a genuine misunderstanding on the part of the customers, who had very little cash and no realisable assets; all they could do in recompense was to return the unused rashers of bacon to the seller.

★ ★ ★

There could not have been many valuables left in the camp by the end of the third year. The camp dentist was kept busy extracting gold fillings and replacing the cavities with dental cement, the gold fillings going for sale.

There was a swap list on the noticeboard: a zip fastener was offered for rice; a pair of platinum earrings with pearls in exchange for two tins of corned beef etc. If you could not sell or swap your goods, the next thing was the Indian Auction. This was held periodically on the green outside the Indian Quarters (where the Indian Prison Warders had lived in peace time), and yielded many bargains.

Luxury articles were generally raffled. We tried to raffle a costly manicure set belonging to Olive which our amah had stuffed among the clothes she took to Olive in the Chinese hotel, but we had chosen a time when there was very little spare money around for non-essentials. After a week's weary canvassing, we had not sold enough chances to justify the raffle, so returned the money to the customers then sadly went to the Commissioner of Police to tell him that the raffle was cancelled. He already had a visitor when I arrived — a wan lady whose face lit up when she saw the manicure set. It turned out that she was trying to buy a present for her daughter's 17th birthday and particularly wanted something special, because of a recent great tragedy. Her husband had been imprisoned in the Gaol by the Japanese, fallen ill and died there. She gladly paid me the value we had set on the manicure set, so once more we were in the money and could shop recklessly at the next canteen opening.

★ ★ ★

And now here we were, making our meagre preparations to celebrate the third Christmas in camp. Parents once more faced the problem of acting Santa to their sometimes sceptical offspring; by the nature of the camp-made presents, it did not need very much observation to realise that Santa Claus himself must be an internee! Gifts had to take the form of some trifle made from pieces of cardboard (from the Red Cross parcels), old material or tin. Cuttings from the khaki jerkins supplied were used to make soft toys, pin cushions, bookmarks or wall tidies with pockets. Olive discovered how to make the kind of wallet which secures a note with a cross-strap when you fold it over, and produced quite a lot of them. The kitchen staff did their best with the rations to hand but, unless one had a spare tin of something saved up, the Christmas meal could hardly be called festive.

Our poverty was of a degree that we had never visualised, compared to those we had pre-war regarded as poverty-stricken. In normal life, a poor person could beg, do a casual job or even sing in the street to gain a few pence. We could do none of those things. Creature comforts such as warm beds, hot baths, decent clothing etc. were things of the past and seemed unreal. We just lived from one day to the next: who knew what wonderful event might not happen tomorrow?

★　★　★

The beginning of 1945 brought a fresh flood of optimistic rumours: that the European war was nearly

214

over; that a Task Force (whatever that was) had landed in the Philippine Islands; that our repatriation was imminent. Then something happened which brought us out of our realm of fantasy to the stark reality of our present plight.

It started on January 15th with an American air raid on Hong Kong. The Japanese sounded the air raid alarm in the camp and we all repaired to our quarters as ordered. This alarm lasted for longer than any previous raid, and although we heard plenty of ack-ack fire and the distant thud of bombs we only saw a few planes in the distance flying very high.

Next day at 8.30 a.m. our guards again sounded the alarm. We were confined to quarters all the morning, listening to the zooming of planes and faint bombing a long way away. During a lull in the activity about noon, Olive and Barbara sped down to the hospital for their afternoon shift. Just after that, a group of planes flew over the camp, very high up, in reassuring numbers. They looked like a shoal of small silver fish in the brilliant sunshine. As we gazed in pride at them, two planes collided. One burst into flames and immediately crashed out of sight behind the hills. The other fell more slowly, enabling two men to bale out. Their parachutes opened and one of the men floated down freely (he was captured by the Japanese, we heard later), but the parachute of the other airman became entangled in the falling plane and he was lost.

Suddenly all was noise and confusion. The planes were directly overhead and diving low. Machine gun fire, the snarling of the planes and the thud of their

215

bombs struck terror in our hearts. No consolation that the attackers were our allies and their targets were guns set up on top of the gaol and a large Japanese ship beached in a nearby bay. Several bombs hit the rocks outside the gaol, shattering windows in the hospital and our blocks. The Japanese were retaliating with machine guns from their camp HQ on the hill, as well as with the guns atop the gaol.

At the first onslaught, we rushed into the hallways and corridors for safety and huddled there listening to what sounded like all hell let loose. We felt the blast of one almighty thud. Someone bravely watching from a front verandah shouted to us that Watanabe, one of the Japanese HQ staff, had gone rushing down to the hospital. Olive and Barbara were there when he arrived to seek medical aid for the internees in one of the bungalows which had been hit by a bomb. Volunteers hurried off with stretchers and found that fourteen of our number had been killed outright; another died before reaching hospital. This Japanese officer, who in ordinary life was a Christian minister, had done untold good in trying to alleviate the plight of prisoners of war. (When the war was over, he learned he had lost two of his family in the Hiroshima atom bomb explosion.)

This sobering experience altered our outlook completely. Hitherto we had thought of release in terms of repatriation or triumphant victory; now we were forced to realise that we were very small cogs in the wheels of war, and would have to take our chance if and when an all-out attack on the Colony was made.

We were near enough to Stanley Fort to be in the path of Japanese shells falling short of their targets, and Allied shells overshooting theirs. Up till now the camp had not been marked as a place of internment. By international law it should have been ringed with perimeter lights, and marked with white crosses large enough to be visible from aircraft. After this dreadful raid, men were detailed to dig a large cross on the grass; this was filled in with kaolin clay, which abounded in the area.

At this time, the Japanese allowed the Roman Catholic Bishop of Hong Kong into camp to visit his flock for the first (and only) time. We gathered to greet this venerable figure with flowing beard. Although he was surrounded by armed Japanese officers, he spoke to us fearlessly about "the day of victory" and gave us words of encouragement. We lay folk were not allowed to speak to him, but our senior priest Father Meyer was permitted to address him with the bodyguards in attendance.

★　★　★

From now on, as unobtrusively as possible in order to avoid panic in the camp and the attentions of the Japanese, our camp officials began to work out plans to help us cope with possible Allied large-scale attacks by sea or air. We had no shelters, and the few anti-blast walls erected against Japanese raids four years earlier had long since been dismantled and put to other uses. The aim was that every group of quarters should be self-reliant, as it could be that we might not be able to venture out of doors to get rations.

Over a period of time, each kitchen gradually built up a stock of gritty biscuits, made by mixing dry ground rice with soya bean flour, baked hard. These were to be our iron rations, and not entrusted to individuals (our authorities evidently bearing in mind the definition of a young internee that "iron rations" were reserve rations kept by those of iron will). Each of us had to hand in an empty tin of stock size, which was filled with biscuits, then the whole block's supply was put under lock and key in the block. Obviously a tin of dry biscuits would not keep one person alive for long, but the hope was that the food would sustain us during an allied attack until we were relieved. Most of us also made a small stock of standby food by baking uncooked rice until it was slightly browned, in which state it could be nibbled if there was nothing else to eat.

When the news went round that the unused latrine trenches had been earmarked for mass graves for camp casualties, we began to dread clear days and moonlight nights which might be the prelude to an invasion.

We observed the activities of Japanese working parties on the nearby hillsides where they were building what appeared to be gun emplacements. From their position, the camp experts declared, they could only take guns which faced our location. Although others scoffed at this, there was the uneasy thought that our captors just might intend to wipe us all out if an attack came.

Air raids were almost a daily occurrence now, although they were in the city and not near us. Our hearts ached for the innocent folk who had to endure them — mainly the Chinese, but also our troops in the military camps in Kowloon.

★　★　★

Just at the right time to raise our low morale, there was another issue of Red Cross parcels. Some of the contents had deteriorated, as these parcels were part of the consignment delivered some two years earlier. However, we were very grateful to get them. For a short time we had delectable extras to cheer up our dull, inadequate rations, but of course they did not last long and soon our spirits sank again. People began to lack the energy and heart to go to concerts and other activities which took them away from their own blocks, not liking the prospect of being marooned indefinitely in some other part of the camp during air raid alarms. Then the entertainers themselves found it difficult to get to rehearsals with the constant air raid alarms paralysing movement from one block to another. (We feared the Japanese as much as the bombs, for the former went berserk if they saw any of us out of doors during an alarm) Even Barbara, who had been enthusiastically organising plays for children all through the years, sighed that she just couldn't do any more.

But nothing could discourage the indefatigable Father Meyer. He arranged a mammoth social for his flock and their friends after Easter. A communal cake was baked, with every participant contributing a tiny amount of one of the ingredients, and a raffle organised to raise funds to provide extra canteen food for the sick. The prizes were all camp-made, the main one being made by our friend Mrs K. Using as a background the material from the khaki jerkins issued earlier on, she embroidered a scene familiar to us all — the seashore near Tweed Bay Hospital, the majestic hills, and a Japanese sentry standing in front of his box near the barbed wire that fringed the rocks. We scoured the camp to beg strands of coloured wool from unravelled garments for Mrs K, and the finished product was the most exquisite piece of embroidery I have ever seen.

★　★　★

Another summer came round — our fourth in Stanley. The air raid alarms continued, but there was no more activity over the camp until late July, when at noon one day, unsignalled by any alarm, a large slow-moving plane flew low over Stanley, dropped several bombs in our midst then moved off seawards. Miraculously and mysteriously, not one of the bombs exploded on impact, although several of them fell on camp quarters and damaged them; thankfully there were no fatalities although several internees were injured. The general opinion was that the whole thing was a stunt on the part of the Japanese, although some people considered the plane might have been in difficulties (it was certainly flying in a laboured way), and had jettisoned its load in a hurry meaning the bombs to go into the sea.

We were given the Japanese version next Friday after roll call. The inspection party stood beside two tables which had been pushed together to form a platform. On one table stood Mr Gimson, the Colonial Secretary and Representative of Internees, with his interpreter — an internee who spoke fluent Japanese. On the other stood Lieutenant Kadowaki, the senior Japanese official in camp, who made a speech in such explosive Japanese that we feared we might be destined for the execution block. The interpreter translated in a whisper to Mr Gimson, who in turn relayed it to us.

First, the Lieutenant expressed his sympathy for the damage to persons and quarters during the recent air raid by an American plane. There was a moment of danger, as a murmur of indignation rose from the assembly. Mr Gimson's calm and emotionless expression conveyed a warning to "cool it" as he continued to speak. Our Japanese officials, he said, considered we had grown careless about bowing to them. The Lieutenant appreciated that our customs were different from theirs, but regretted he would have to take action (unspecified) if we did not mend our ways. So that there could be no doubt about our duties in the matter, the Lieutenant detailed a Japanese guard to mount the table to demonstrate:

a) how to bow to a soldier who was wearing a hat, and

b) how to bow to soldier who was not wearing a hat.

221

We dared not laugh, but were greatly relieved that the angry speech in Japanese had been on such a minor matter. Probably none of the offended Japanese officers realised that our reluctance to bow was not so much that we felt it undignified as that we felt plain daft doing it!

We could never have guessed it at the time, but that was our last roll call. There were plenty of optimistic rumours about the progress of the Allies, but remembering the waiting trenches and grim emergency plans, our hopes for release were still tempered with apprehension about how it might be achieved.

★ ★ ★

A few days later, the Japanese asked for the names of all technicians in camp. Why? There were plenty of rumours. One was that there was to be an exchange of British internee technicians for Japanese ones held in Allied countries; another, that the Japanese needed help in town to run essential services.

Once they had registered their names, the technicians were given exactly three hours to get ready to leave camp with wives and families. In that time two marriages were solemnised, but the new brides were not allowed to accompany their husbands, although a Japanese official told one of the girls that she might be able to join her husband in ten days' time — and he was not far out.

We gathered around the railings of the Married Quarters to watch those 177 souls assembling on the road below us. Neither they nor we knew their destination, but it became clear that they were heading for the jetty, so a sea journey was involved. Most were dressed in the best they had; even though it was high summer, one little girl had squeezed into the thick serge coat she had worn coming into camp three years earlier. Everyone carried something — baskets, basins, and suitcases and bags hooked coolie fashion on poles. Not without misgivings, we watched them trail out of sight, then hurried back to ransack the dustbins to see whether anyone had discarded anything of use.

★ ★ ★

A strong rumour was circulating that Russia had declared war on Japan; it was even being said that Japan was about to surrender. Much as we would have liked to believe these tales, we knew better than to treat them seriously. Yet there had been an unusual incident not long ago. Used as we were to total blackouts, we were amazed late one night to find our room suddenly flooded with reflected lights from the jail below us. We got out of bed and could see several cars with bright headlights entering the main gate, while a radio loudspeaker blared noisily (but unrecognisably to us). The optimists thought this could only mean that the end of the war was near. The Black Market, which up to now had dealt only in gold, jewellery and watches, now became wide open for almost any item, from fur coats to a pair of stockings; the general inference was

223

that people in the know in town were now desperate to get rid of all their Japanese yen before the war ended.

Even the most sceptical of us were beginning to allow ourselves to believe the war was over, when on August 14th a lone plane swooped over Tweed Bay near the hospital and attacked a small Japanese craft. There was no air raid alarm and everyone was taken unawares; swimmers rushed out of the water, gardeners popped out of their hillside plots, children playing around shrieked. We all dashed for cover, huddling together while the plane zoomed to and fro and attacked the ship again. The Japanese at headquarters fired their rifles every time the plane flew near. When all was quiet again, we emerged to find that neither casualties nor damage had been caused in the camp. The plane had done what it had evidently come to do — sink an enemy craft which was reputedly working on a boom.

But not only were our nerves badly shaken: gone were our hopes that the war was over.

★ ★ ★

Two days later, August 16th, we were flabbergasted by a messenger charging through the corridors shouting "The war's over; all go down for your Victory roll!"

Though convinced the whole thing was a joke, we hurried downstairs to investigate. A long queue had already formed, and a real toilet roll was being handed to each person — the first ever during internment. Now we were ready to believe anything!

224

There was no official announcement, but all day victory rumours gathered strength, and the camp seethed with cautious excitement. There was much coming and going of Japanese officials in lorries from headquarters.

Suddenly a strange sound was heard — the ringing bells of a fire engine! We rushed to the railings surrounding our block from where we could see the main road. Incredibly, there WAS a fire engine. Manning it were some of the technicians who had been taken from camp ten days ago — one of them belonged to the pre-war Fire Brigade. They confirmed that the war was indeed over.

When we were not summoned for the usual Friday roll call, at last we dared to believe it. At noon a representative of the camp council visited each block in turn and read a statement that hostilities had ceased, the terms of the Potsdam Conference having been accepted. We were advised to be prudent and cautious in our celebrations until the arrival of the relieving forces, as the situation might well be tense for the next few days while we were still in Japanese hands.

The first reaction of those who had any reserves of tinned food was to wade into them. The girls and I had long since used up our little hoard (apart from the siege rice) but generous neighbours gave us some sugar, a tin of bully beef and two sweet potatoes. Gardeners rushed out and dug up everything that was anywhere ready to eat. From the communal store we were each given our tin of siege biscuits, some cheap washing soap and a

225

small portion of corned beef. Altogether, that day it seemed like Christmas!

The Japanese reconnected the electricity and that night the lights of Stanley shone again. It was astonishing to find how unsatisfactory artificial light seemed at first, and as for Henry the cat, who had never seen electric light before, he just sat on the bed and gazed about him in sheer astonishment.

We had been warned by our authorities not to attempt to leave the camp until we were handed over to our forces, so obediently stayed put, but soon the outside world came to visit us. More of the technicians who had been taken from camp returned, and we learned that they and the rest of the band had certainly gone farther and fared worse: after an uncomfortable sea trip in a junk, they had been housed in leaking dilapidated huts in Kowloon, fed on spinach and rice, and the menfolk required to cut barbed wire.

Other visitors came by sea — the sampan people who lived on their little boats. A fleet of them came inshore with fish, eggs and bananas for sale and barter. It was good to see these sunburnt folk again, and in spite of their gaunt and haggard appearance, they grinned cheerfully as they haggled and struck bargains with us. They would take practically any item for their wares as they did not expect us to have cash. I traded some rice and old clothes for seven bananas, and my heavy winter coat for four duck eggs, two crabs and some fish.

After a few days when there was no sign of our relieving forces, Mr Gimson bravely took matters into his own hands, demanded transport from the Japanese camp officials, and went in to town to set up a temporary administration pending the arrival of the Allied Fleet. He took with him a skeleton staff, and never was a description more apt. Our Police Force also left Stanley to maintain law and order in town. From then on we were sent supplies of such forgotten delights as cube sugar, tinned milk, coffee and margarine. There was fresh excitement every day, helping to make this waiting period in camp more bearable. Three British officers from the Kowloon camps arrived by launch, bringing the first real uncensored letters from husbands, sons and friends. The officers said the men would be able to visit Stanley in batches of a hundred or so, as soon as transport could be arranged. How thrilling it was the day the first ferryload was sighted approaching the jetty! Everyone surged down to the water's edge to watch them come ashore, although no one knew whether their particular loved one would be there. The visitors were wearing the remnants of their uniforms, carefully hoarded against just this day; their pockets were bulging with tins or packets of food which they distributed freely.

Lorryloads and launchloads of troops now came every day, but they had to go back to their camps before dark every evening. Two weeks after the surrender, there was still no sign of the expected Fleet. We sometimes felt a little apprehensive; surely by now some envoy should have flown in to reassure us? We stood endlessly staring out to sea hoping to see ships;

scanned the skies for planes, expecting leaflets might be dropped.

The first intimation that we had not been forgotten by the outside world was when a visitor from town brought us a leaflet addressed to all prisoners of war from General Wedemeyer telling us to stay in the camps until the arrival of the Fleet. At last we had something definite to go on and we waited with renewed hope.

Already we were a changed camp — no rumours now, everything was fact. If someone popped his head round your door and said, "Cube sugar, twenty lumps each," you knew it was true and went down to the queue to collect it. Sweets were sent in for the children. Fresh meat had been unearthed from cold storage, the stews now tasted and smelled like stew instead of garbage water. In fact, much of the daily rice ration was uneaten as we no longer needed it for a filler, so every evening the surplus cooked rations were taken by volunteers to the Carmelite Convent in Stanley Village. Here the Sisters distributed it among the orphans in the convent and the crowds of fisher folk. It made our hearts ache to see the gaunt, skeletal forms of these poor people. We internees had at least had our two meals daily, however scant, but they had had to fend entirely for themselves.

Our dustbins were overflowing with empty tins, banana and orange skins. The corridors were heavy with the heavenly aroma of coffee. We were no longer hungry for food — only for news. Without the Japanese to worry about our morals, a dance was held in St Stephen's Hall. (Dancing had been frowned on as very immoral by our captors.) Not minding the intense heat and the enormous crush, everyone enjoyed shuffling round the floor with a partner, just because it had been forbidden for years. During the evening, someone turned up with a radio. We all surged round to listen to the delightful oscillations which meant that we were at last about to hear something direct from the outside world. Though reception was very poor, we were thrilled to the marrow to hear a news summary directed to prisoners of war.

After this, radio bulletins were posted daily on our notice boards. We read about atom bombs dropped on Japan and wondered about them, and the many wives who knew their husbands had been sent to Japan were sick with anxiety in case they had been victims of the new bombs. Repatriation was always in the news, but still no Fleet came.

We didn't take too seriously a report that a plane would drop parachute supplies over Stanley on August 29th, especially as the appointed day was overcast and rainy. Nevertheless, everyone came out of their rooms and watched the skies — and the fairytale came true! Out of the low grey clouds it came, flying slowly towards the camp, so low that we could see the first packages being pushed out from the plane's belly. As with one voice, the watching crowds sighed in ecstasy at the beauty of the parachutes as they opened and floated gracefully down — green, red, blue and white — shouting encouragement as their burden swayed towards the Indian Quarters green; howled with disappointment when one was wafted into the bay;

229

palpitated as the plane appeared to hit the high land beyond the camp perimeter, then breathed again as it rose safely and turned again for another run in.

The contents of the huge green canisters — cigarettes, medical and food supplies — didn't go very far between so many, but no matter; this was the reassurance we had needed, and morale shot sky high.

Word went round that day that the Fleet was near. We gazed seawards until nightfall, almost cross-eyed by that time, but in vain. Next morning the Fleet rumours were even stronger, and crowds of people hied themselves up to the rooftops the better to scan the horizon. To reach the roof of our block, one had to climb a vertical iron ladder leading to a trap door. The roof was a favourite haunt for coolness during the hot evenings, but the girls had begged me never to attempt this dangerous climb, and I had promised I would not try it until Victory Day. Now the great day had come, so up I went.

CHAPTER
SIX

Afterwards

It was a perfect summer's morning. The sky and the hills were all before us in the most glorious technicolour that only Nature can produce. Around 8 a.m., into this glorious scene darted a number of planes, and then the Fleet — our Navy — sailed grandly into sight; in the far distance the ships continued purposefully on their course towards the harbour entrance, then were lost to our sight. But they were there! The Fleet was in! We were practically free!

The planes now began to fly back and forth over the camp to greet us, some dropping packets of cigarettes. In the middle of all these thrills, Barbara was notified to be ready to leave Stanley that afternoon to join the Colonial Secretary's staff in town. We carried her folded camp bed and meagre belongings down to the ration dump to await the promised transport. It happened to be Mabel's birthday, and a party had been planned for the evening. We brought Barbara's share of the party food to her and she ate it sitting on her suitcase at the roadside, in prime position to see a car drive through the gates; out stepped the civil servant internee who was our camp commandant now the Colonial Secretary was in town.

"The Admiral will be here in a few minutes," he announced. "Tell everyone you see and get them to assemble outside the Married Quarters."

Everyone in hearing dashed off shouting the glad tidings — everyone except Barbara, who dared not move from the spot in case her transport arrived; she was frantic with frustration lest it should do so before the entry of the relieving forces which she couldn't bear to miss.

People flocked from all corners of the camp, and it was every man for himself to secure the best vantage points. Roofs and verandahs of the blocks overlooking the Married Quarters were soon filled to capacity, and the grass below was a seething mass of happy people.

Suddenly, through the camp gates drove two large shiny cars carrying the Admiral and his retinue, all grossly overdressed by our standards! Immediately behind came several open vehicles (jeeps) the like of which we had never seen; they were filled with large blooming men with cheeks so ruddy that they seemed to us to be wearing stage makeup; all in whiter-than-white tropical kit, they looked far too clean and dressed up to be real. What they in turn thought of us at first sight, heaven only knows.

The Admiral made a short speech, the National Anthem was sung and the Union Jack hoisted. What a moment! I am sure a prayer of thankfulness went up from every heart. Then the flags of every other nation represented in the camp were hoisted, even a Greek flag by the only such national in camp.

The Admiral and his party left, then the Captain of HMS *Maidstone* arrived in another strange vehicle, a "dukw", and gave a breezy description of world events leading up to the surrender. While he was addressing us, the rating left in charge of the dukw was having a hectic time with the camp youngsters who, intrigued by this vehicle from another world, were in it, on it, and even under it.

Meanwhile a dilapidated old bus with a hole in the floor and no glass in its windows turned up to take Barbara and several other people into town; she was a little sad at having to miss the camp's celebrations of liberty, but told me later that being in an office at the rebirth of the administration was the most exciting thing she had ever experienced.

★ ★ ★

Stanley celebrated in style that night. Mabel's boyfriend, Clifton, and his friends humped an old, small harmonium from the recreation room to our room for Mabel's party. Many of the notes didn't play but I managed to grind out *Twenty-one today*. The fact that she was 22 didn't matter at all. When we heard that a naval guard had arrived to police the camp perimeter and that some of the detail were off duty, Mabel and Clifton went off to invite one or two to the party. They returned triumphantly with one very shy young sailor — only one because it seemed the boys were in great demand and were almost being press-ganged into attending parties throughout the camp. Of course, every one was avid for news of the outside world, and here was a chance of getting some first hand.

Our festive board did not seem to appeal much to our guest. It was not until a week later after we ourselves had tasted civilised meals again that we realised that corned beef sandwiches (the bread a doughy Chinese product cooked without salt brought in from town), and rice-flour pancakes could hardly have had the same attraction for him as for us.

Next Naval photographers arrived and took pictures throughout the camp. Small naval craft anchored in Tweed Bay opposite the hospital and the Navy invited internees to visit the ships via liberty boats.

Olive joined Barbara in the Government offices in town, and now events began to shape up for our release. First, all the sick and ailing were taken on board a hospital ship which sailed for Australia. Mabel and I were among the large majority detailed for the next ship expected, but Olive and Barbara at their own request were listed for deferred repatriation. Though working very hard at their typewriters during the day, they were having a whale of a time every evening, as block invitations were always arriving for ships' parties etc. They were finding clothes rather a problem, as the promised Red Cross supplies had not yet materialised and there were practically no European clothes in the few shops that were open even if you had the money to buy them. The Government workers received a small advance on salary, but it bore little relation to the astronomical prices prevailing.

No one could tell us what date we — Mabel and I — would be leaving Hong Kong, but I was anxious to see the other two girls before sailing, so got permission to go into town in an old bus which bumped over the familiar roads. It was sad to see the former beautiful shrubs and bushes grown completely wild; the wholesale felling for firewood of young trees, so carefully planted and tended by the pre-war Forestry Department, had left ugly scars on the hillside.

When I met up with Olive and Barbara, we climbed aboard an old green tram to Happy Valley to visit Will's grave. Our flat was nearby so we went to see it. Although the block had suffered from bombing, our flat was not demolished. What the bombs had not fully accomplished, the looters had. We picked our way gingerly up the stairs from which every vestige of wood had been removed. Our front door too had gone — we walked straight through to a scene of desolation. The place had been entirely stripped, floorboards and all. A dusty parchment lampshade and a broken plant pot containing the ghost of my beautiful pink camellia were the only things left to convince us we had ever lived there.

This visit disposed of our favourite pipe dream in camp — that of returning to the city and finding our homes just as we had left them at the outbreak of war. In fact, a few people did find their homes intact because Chinese or third national friends had taken them over before the Japanese arrived, and looked after them, but the majority of us had to face the fact that our earthly possessions were gone for ever. Not that this worried us over much at the time; to recover one's pre-war home would just have been an added bonus to the wonderful gift of survival and freedom.

The girls put me up overnight in their billet, as I intended to spend all the next day — Sunday — with them. After Mass at St Joseph's (the Church miraculously undamaged, although the church hall twenty yards away had been bombed flat), we heard a rumour that the *Empress of Australia* was due to sail from Stanley the next day. I got myself back to camp post haste, taking with me a most painful pair of feet after all the unaccustomed walking on hard pavements in old shoes.

Mabel was nearly frantic when I returned, in case I had not heard about the scheduled embarkation and decided to stay a second night in town. Everyone was busily packing, going through their belongings and throwing out what had been treasured possessions.

Up at the crack of dawn next day, we dumped our bug-ridden bedding on to a great bonfire in the courtyard. Henry the cat was handed over to a lady missionary who promised him a home with friends in Hong Kong, and I heard later that he had settled down there well. Knowing that Olive and Barbara were well and happy and would be following us to England shortly, there was nothing to mar for me the magic moment of leaving Stanley. In spite of privations, my family and I had been happy, we had been together and we had survived. Certainly at times we had thought our lot hard, but when in England we heard the stories of Belsen and Dachau, well, I began to wonder whether we had had much to moan about after all.

Small craft ferried us from the jetty to the huge ship awaiting us out in the bay. And then we were treading the deck of that ship — long dreamed about — which would take us to freedom and our homeland.

Many men from the military camps were already aboard, but the best accommodation had been kept for women and children. Mabel and I and eight acquaintances were sent to an airy cabin on A deck which we learned had been part of the Royal Suite occupied by King George VI and Queen Elizabeth on their pre-war trip to Canada. Of course extra bunks had now been fitted, but the overcrowding didn't worry any of us. The deep, sprung mattresses, the crisp white sheets and plump pillows looked so inviting that we could hardly wait to go to bed that first night.

As for the meals in the huge, ornate dining saloon, they became the highlights of each day. We stuffed ourselves with bread rolls and butter between courses, still finding it hard to believe that the roll basket would be refilled whenever it became empty. Not all the young children shared our enthusiasm for what to them were new foods, many clamouring for rice.

One day a friend and I were leaning over the ship's rail when a whole consignment of rolls came flying out of a galley porthole into the sea. "A month ago we'd have gone over the side after that lot," said my companion.

There were film shows in the evenings, but we found it hard to follow the stories; all the characters looked gross and overdressed, and their electronic voices sounded harsh and the music raucous to our unaccustomed ears. It was the same with the radio programmes, everyone seemed to speak too quickly and too loudly. No doubt our powers of concentration were somewhat weakened.

Our immediate destination was not announced, but we didn't worry very much as long as it was in the direction of freedom. Came one evening when the *Empress of Australia* steamed slowly into what looked like a graveyard of ships — Manila harbour. Wrecks of large vessels, both American and Japanese, were everywhere, many of them sitting squarely on the sea-bed with just masts and superstructure showing. Once alongside a mangled, shattered wharf, our service personnel were disembarked and taken to a rest camp for a fortnight's recuperation before final repatriation. At this camp our troops met up with other Hong Kong prisoners of war shipped to Japan in 1942 who had just been flown from Japan to Manila. Among them were seven who learned from the Empress arrivals that their wives and children were aboard our ship; of course, these seven men were at the dockside in no time, and seven lucky women — who had thought their husbands were in Japan if they had survived at all — heard their names called over the ship's radio at midnight and were told to report forthwith to the forward gangway where their husbands awaited them.

Next day the *Empress* moved out into the harbour and anchored to a large wreck used as a buoy. Here we sat in the fierce September sun for a whole week, after which a large contingent of troops who had already had their fortnight's rest in the camp ashore were brought aboard and the ship sailed again. There were more joyful reunions with old friends. Mabel met up with a number of ex-patients from the Military Hospital, and for the next few days I was always being introduced to this one and that one who had been her patients, until I began to think she had nursed the entire Hong Kong forces.

A day out of Manila we civilians were summoned to the main recreation room for the distribution of secondhand clothing taken on in port. Tables were piled high with garments of every description and we were told to help ourselves. The scene at a London bargain basement sale was beaten to a frazzle by what went on in that room! The frantic scramble to the tables, the grabbing of likely-looking articles, then hanging on to them while trying another garment on, was unforgettable. No matter that they were somebody else's cast-offs, they were something different from the faded rags we had been wearing for so long. The troops on the deck watching through the windows declared that the whole thing beat any entertainment they had ever seen.

Next stop was Singapore and here there was another passenger re-shuffle. Men whose wives were in Australia, and some internees in poor health, were transferred to a hospital ship bound for Australia and

New Zealand. As in Manila, the rest of us were not allowed ashore, but no one minded — we were only interested in getting HOME.

★ ★ ★

This journey, never knowing exactly where we were going or who we would meet on the way, was full of the unexpected, and I was in for a real surprise when we tied up in Colombo harbour on October 2nd. The first tender alongside brought Mabel's fiancé, Clifton, whom she had left behind in Hong Kong three weeks earlier. Nor was that all — he told us that Olive and Barbara were also in Colombo! They had left Hong Kong nine days ago with a few hundred other ex-internees on a fast aircraft carrier and had reached Colombo the previous day. Clifton's one idea was to marry Mabel right away for, as he was Canadian, he feared he might be sent to Canada, and wanted to make sure Mabel went with them. The two had been keen to marry for the last two years but I had insisted they wait until they were out of camp.

Now they were scouring the ship for a priest. Next, I heard a broadcast over the tannoy asking Father James to go to cabin 8 (ours). I begged the excited pair to wait a little longer and have the wedding when times were more normal and settled — but in vain. "You said we could marry when we got out," Mabel reminded me. "Well, here we are, out!"

The priest arrived and asked me to find two witnesses. Mabel's wedding finery consisted of just the

240

clothes she was wearing — a white silk blouse made out of one of my petticoats, a pair of shorts, and no socks or stockings — just sandals made from some old crepe rubber with bands of khaki material. Clifton wore shorts and shirt, on which latter Mabel insisted on sewing a missing button, even though it delayed the ceremony. Not many brides can claim to have been married in a royal suite, using a hollowed-out coin as a wedding ring, and wearing clothes more suited to the beach than a wedding!

Before I could recover my wits, the newlyweds had gone blissfully down the gangway as man and wife to Clifton's billet ashore. Shortly after I was summoned to the main gangway where stood Olive and Barbara (almost unrecognisable in new clothes) arguing with officialdom to be allowed on board to see me. With three friends they had hired a small boat to get to the ship. They hadn't a pass between them and it was some time before they were allowed on board. They had been billeted with some Colombo residents who had been family friends of ours and who had recognised the surname on the list of arrivals and offered them private accommodation. In the odd way that things happened, they had already bumped into Clifton and Mabel in the town.

"Hey, we're married!" Mabel called to them, while Clifton nodded in dazed confirmation.

Barbara applied to take over Mabel's bunk in cabin 8 and travel Home with me. (She and Olive had been sleeping with others in hammocks four deep on the aircraft carrier — our cabin on the *Empress* was sheer luxury compared with that.) What was in effect a simple swap turned out to need much paperwork ashore, but after hitch-hiking around Colombo that day Barbara managed at length to track down the right official in some obscure office who gave the necessary permission.

Meanwhile, we other passengers were taken ashore in relays to be given VIP treatment by the Red Cross. As we went in buses from the jetty to the Red Cross centre we passed through a wealthy residential area and feasted our eyes on palatial homes in tropical surroundings. A child behind me was particularly taken by one such house set in velvety lawns.

"Oh Mummy, look at that lovely house!" she piped. "You always said we would live in a nice house with a garden when we get out of camp — let's live in that one!

★　★　★

The Red Cross centre was at Echelon Barracks and here innumerable delights awaited us. Not only were we ladies fitted out with skirts and blouses (used but greatly welcomed) but we could avail ourselves of hot baths and beauty treatment, including hair-dos. There were opticians and dentists to attend to us. I had an eye test, as my glasses had been useless for a long time, and by the next day a new pair of glasses was ready for me. Children wandered, but a loudhailer soon found them again.

242

Among the milling hundreds of ex-prisoners of war (or RAPWI as we found we were officially termed) I came across Clifton and Mabel, the latter looking quite a stranger in her new wardrobe. She told me how well she had been treated by helpers in the clothing tent when they heard she had just been married. The best clothes were selected and handed for her to try on but, anxious though she was to do so, she had hesitated because she was wearing such peculiar underwear.

"I just held each dress up against me," she related, and at last one of the older helpers guessed her embarrassment and told her not to worry, that they had seen some odd sights on this job. When she undressed and stood there in a bra made from Clifton's scout kerchief (one cup blue, one cup yellow) and panties made from old mosquito net reinforced in the seat with a square of a flour bag — complete with faded lettering, the helpers struggled to look polite, but it was no good: one giggle from Mabel at their contorted faces sent them all into peals of laughter.

When the *Empress of Australia* sailed out of Colombo, she carried a very contented load of people, all resplendent in clothes which completely put in the shade the garments previously received on board. But the Red Cross had not finished with us! Some days later the ship dropped anchor at Adibaya, near Suez. Adibaya seemed to be just a barren strip of desert with a backdrop of coffee-coloured hills, bare and heavily ridged, but the picture ashore was very different. Everything had been done to try and put a welcome into the arid desert scene — even the highest cranes were decorated with strings of gay little flags.

At the RAF camp a hanger had been converted into a rest room, with carpeted floor, bunting-covered tables and deep cushioned easy chairs. Every table had a spent shell case holding bright flowers. A fenced nursery kept the small children happy with rocking horses, see-saws and little swings. Enormous cream cakes, piles of sandwiches and tea and soft drinks were pressed on us while we waited our turn to be fitted out with even more clothes — new ones this time!

This operation took place in an adjoining hanger fitted out like a department store. By the time we had passed through every department, we each had one of everything to wear from top to toe, plus a large canvas hold-all for our spoils. In every way we were treated more like wealthy customers instead of penniless refugees. Since we were taken ashore in ordered batches, there was a lot of waiting time on board until every single one of us had been kitted out; in that 48 hours ENSA boarded the *Empress* and provided all kinds of entertainment, an RAF band introducing us to the latest dance music.

After Suez we hit rough weather. One strict rule had been that all ladies must be out of the public rooms and off the decks by 10 p.m. Authority regularly reminded us of the rule over the tannoy, with additional reproaches for those who did not obey promptly. The bad weather sent most of us reeling to our cabins long before the deadline. On the worst night, when the voice over the tannoy announced "It is 10 p.m." there was no reminder that it was bedtime; instead, just a sympathetic "Good night, ladies."

* * *

We anchored off the Mersey in gale force winds one October evening. Next day the gale was still raging so we had to face another 24 hours rocking at anchor. Frustrating though this was, we could at least see England now, and on grey choppy seas, a sky full of screaming gulls, and green hills in the misty distance, we feasted our impatient eyes.

What a wonderful welcome we had as we thronged the decks when at last the *Empress* crept past the guiding buoys to Liverpool! Small ferries circled as near as they dared, their passengers calling out the names of relatives and friends they had come to meet. Hundreds of people on the docks stood on a raised platform, cheering and waving. Many held aloft banners of welcome and personal messages for individuals. Hooters hooted, whistles shrilled, and a band was playing on the dockside. In the midst of all this excitement, a voice over the tannoy managed to make itself heard: "Will the troops on E deck please go below and clear up their quarters?"

Needless to say, with all there was to watch, no one left the upper decks. The message was repeated twice, then a third time with the variation that no troops would be allowed to disembark until the order was carried out. Presently, from our grandstand on the promenade deck, we saw a shower of articles coming

245

through the portholes of E deck — E deck was being cleared with a vengeance!

A launch drew alongside with a group of funereal-looking gentlemen, all with bowler hats, rolled umbrellas and brief-cases. We had forgotten that this was normal apparel for city workers, and could hardly keep straight faces as they filed up the gangway. But they all turned out to be charming and helpful officials when we met them later that day in the recreation lounge. Some were from the Passport Office and dealt with our papers. An Accommodation Officer had records from which he could tell each one of us exactly where we were to go once disembarked, friends and relatives having notified this department where they had room for the arrivals. Those with no close relatives in this country learned that accommodation had been arranged for them in a hostel in Coventry. Such was the prevailing spirit of hospitality then that Barbara and I had the offers of two homes with friends, in addition to that from my sisters in Gillingham, our chosen destination. There was a railway official to provide us with travel warrants, and a Post Office official to despatch telegrams we wrote out to let relatives know times of arrival at destinations; nothing had been forgotten or left to chance. As everyone of us had to pass through the hands of all these officials, the procedure went on well into the evening, and Barbara and I were among hundreds who had to spend yet another night on board.

Somehow we managed to sleep a little that night. Somehow we managed to suppress the desire to leap into the air and scream loud hallelujahs as we trooped down the gangway, each armed with farewell handouts of chocolates, cigarettes and a picnic bag of sausage rolls and cakes.

We were taken first to a baggage room to identify our luggage, which had been landed overnight. This was no easy task, since all 3,000 of us possessed identical canvas bags supplied in Adibaya! Then Barbara and I and all those bound for London were led to a train at Riverside Station. Throughout the long journey south we stared out of the windows, drinking in scenes we had never thought to see again, and the dull autumn weather did nothing to dampen our spirits; we were free, once more in our homeland, and on our way to meet our nearest and dearest — we had all the sunshine in our hearts.

And so on to Euston Station. From the waiting crowds on the platform, my sister Lilian's anxious face emerged. Obviously she was uncertain whether the madly waving figure in thick khaki slacks and scarlet jacket was Barbara, but when I appeared too, there was no doubt in her face. We hugged, we wept, we laughed and wept again.

An official directed us to a waiting ambulance, which took us, and a little family who were dropped off en route, to Gillingham. To see again that familiar little front garden in Sunnymead Avenue brought a wave of happiness that was almost unbearable. Another sister welcomed us indoors. Lilian's husband (now aged eighty) was waiting at the railway station in case we arrived by train, and had been there for hours. The ambulance drivers (all volunteers) immediately drove to the station and brought him home, then we all, drivers included, sat down to a sumptuous meal of ox tongue. "The butcher let us have a whole one to celebrate your homecoming," Lilian said.

Nothing can ever quite surpass the joy of a homecoming. Lilian took us to the local shops and introduced us, as all the friendly assistants had been told about our prospective arrival. Lilian and her husband produced special little luxuries they had been hoarding against our return. And I really felt I was not dreaming it all when I was handed my share of the recent summer crop of lavender from the faithful old family bush.

★   ★   ★

Rationing and left-over war restrictions had made England a very different place from the England we had left in 1938. There were times when I felt like Rip Van Winkle, such as the first time I went to the post office with a sheaf of letters and asked for the requisite number of three halfpenny stamps. The young assistant seemed unduly interested as I affixed the stamps, then said, "You will need two penny-ha'penny stamps on those letters, dear, you know."

As ex-internees we were given extra food coupons to help combat our malnutrition, and extra clothing coupons to build up our wardrobes. I immediately bought myself some knitting wool and decided to knit two jumpers at once, each on alternate days, so as to have both finished at the same time. I chose quite elaborate patterns and they began to look highly attractive, but as time went on I began to wonder whether I was fighting a losing battle. As the jumpers grew in length, so I grew in width with the regular and nourishing meals. When finished the jumpers looked as smart as I had visualised — but not for me: I had to sell them to someone with lesser dimensions and start again.

Olive arrived in England a few weeks after Barbara and I, closely followed by Mabel and her husband who had not been sent to Canada after all. Yet, despite our joy and relief at reaching England, there was a vague feeling of restlessness, of not belonging. Perhaps it was the onset of the British winter; perhaps the peculiar fascination Hong Kong seems to have, so that Europeans always seem reluctant to leave it for ever. Whatever the reason, by the end of the next year — 1946 — the girls and I were all back in Hong Kong again — Olive and Barbara and Clifton resuming their pre-war jobs, and Mabel busy with her first baby. My idea was to make a home for the two older girls, but at this time flats were scarcer than diamonds and almost as expensive; most Europeans were destined to live in hostels or hotels for some time to come, so instead I took a post as manageress of a hostel, very near to a similar hostel where Olive and Barbara were accommodated. Every ship brought back a trickle to swell the number of camp acquaintances who admired each other's newly acquired curves — and were forever a race apart, sharing a memory that still occasionally colours our attitude towards such things as wasted crusts, comfortable beds, and cups of tea ad lib.

In the course of time both Olive and Barbara married, and I welcomed nine grandchildren, all of whom spent most of their early years in Hong Kong. In 1954 I decided the time had come for me to return to England for good, as my sister Lilian was ailing. Just before I left, Olive took me on an unforgettable cruise to Japan. In the midst of all the wonderful things and places we saw, and the pleasant Japanese folk we met, it seemed incredible that we had less than ten years earlier regarded Japan as our deadly enemy.

I settled down in Kent with my sisters and brother-in-law — all much older than myself. Almost every year one or other of the girls and families came Home on leave with the excitement of reunion. Barbara, husband and family spent one leave in Scotland and I lived with them there for six months, visiting some of the places Will and I had known in our early married life, and renewing acquaintances with the few of our friends who were still living in the district.

When Lilian and her huband died, the girls invited me back to Hong Kong so once again I found myself on a P & O ship headed East. That really was my last trip, because the following year Barbara's husband retired to settle in England; I was content to return too, now I had some family near at hand. So back to Kent again, now to look after my surviving sister.

I had a holiday in Sussex with Olive and her family when they came on leave, and distinguished myself by breaking a leg; as a result I spent four weeks decorating

250

the only downstairs room of their delightful "ye olde" cottage with me and my bed which had to be brought downstairs. The frustration of just lying there in plaster when I was supposed to be on a visit was bad enough, but once I was home again in Kent, getting about on crutches was even worse.

"You need exercises," said the doctor. These were to take place at a hospital eight miles away, whither I was to be taken daily by ambulance. Came the first morning, and I was most apprehensive about how I would manage when the ambulance attendants tried to lift my great weight down the steps from the house to the road, as I could not negotiate the steps on crutches. I need not have worried.

"Put your arms round our necks, love, don't be shy," said the senior attendant.

At the hospital I was trundled by wheelchair to the gymnasium and given half an hour's instruction on how to exercise the knee muscles. This was both difficult and painful, but it was encouraging and interesting to watch the other patients doing various exercises for their particular disabilities.

Next I was taken to the Occupational Therapy Department next door, and beheld what appeared to be a hive of industry. An attractive young woman took charge of me and said I was to do some weaving. I sincerely hope my face didn't register my thoughts — disgust at having been brought eight miles to do weaving when I had as much needlework and knitting on hand at home to fill my time for weeks. But when I found myself sitting at a loom, with my leg in a sling

251

and the foot attached to a pulley, I had to re-organise my ideas. The aim was to reduce the excessive swelling around the ankle. The heddle of the loom was raised and lowered by the pointing of the toe to its fullest extent and then returning it to its normal position. The shuttle I used with my hands. The whole operation was slow as it took real effort to raise and lower the heddle. I only managed about eight rows, three of which I had to undo, as I had lifted the heddle when I should have lowered it and thus changed the weave.

Each succeeding morning the movements became easier and the swelling gradually reduced. In due course the leg was slung in a different position so that I had to stretch and bend the knee to manipulate the heddle.

The many varied activities of my fellow patients really amazed me. Arthritics were making baskets and stools with rushes and cane, and turning out really professional work. One lady, very badly crippled with arthritis in both hips, had a bed-loom on which she made beautiful stoles.

There were printing machines which could be fixed to be worked by the hand, for arm exercises, or, as in my case, by foot. I was put on a stationary bicycle with a fretsaw attached for a spell. As I pedalled, so the little saw worked. When I remarked to the man in charge that there was a lot of good energy going to waste, he gave me a piece of wood marked with pencil lines, fixed it in position and said, "Pedal away, and let's see if you can cut a straight line."

I managed fairly well, so was then given cuts of plywood, marked out for the bases of the baskets. My pedalling produced bases which were a bit wavy round the edges, but this did not matter too much as the edges had to be sandpapered afterwards — as I soon found out when I was transferred to the sanding machine. There, my feet were strapped to a treadle which worked sideways and pulled a block of sandpaper to and fro over the shaped basket bases and made them beautifully smooth.

There seemed no end to the gadgets both for working and playing. Yes, even games were provided to give weakened muscles the movement they needed: puff billiards played with rubber bulbs and featherweight balls, and bagatelle to strengthen damaged fingers. Two totally blind patients were expert at basket-making. It was marvellous to see one of them leave the work table, go to the store shelf and select the length of rattan he wanted for the hanks; he then returned to the table, took a small rule from his pocket and, by the raised studs on the rule, measured the length he needed for the basket strands and from this carefully cut the whole length into equal pieces.

Thanks to the splendid and kindly staff of the Occupational Therapy Department, and the willing and cheerful ambulance men, my leg became almost normal again. I was most grateful too for the experience of seeing the wonderful methods and appliances used so cleverly for the benefit of sufferers.

★ ★ ★

After my remaining sister died, I moved to Somerset to be near Barbara and family, the other two girls being still in Hong Kong. In a delightful village a few miles from them, I bought a lovely little modern house — the sort Will and I had dreamed of having — and spent eight years there in a very happy, friendly community.

In 1971 Barbara and family and I moved to Sussex, where by this time Olive and family had settled on retirement. My little bungalow is only a mile from Olive's home; Barbara and family are only a short train journey away. Mabel and Clifton settled in Australia on retirement, and write frequently. With a loving family — now including three great-grandchildren — a circle of friends with whom I play bridge, and the absorbing pleasure writing these memories has given me, I really thought all my excitements were behind me. But they weren't!

★　★　★

My heart began to give trouble, and after a collapse, the doctor said I should go to hospital for observation.

"I hope you're not going to try to fix me up with a new heart at my time of life," I said (I was nearing my 78th birthday).

"No, not a new one," he replied, "but have you ever heard of a pacemaker?"

I was whisked off by ambulance to hospital and examined and cross-examined. Yes, a pacemaker could be fitted if I agreed to the operation, which I did. This was to take place in a different hospital, but first I was wired up to a machine brought to the bedside, and yards of information taped out on rolls of paper. Then, still wired up to a monitoring machine, I was put into an ambulance and driven to the second hospital and taken straight to the operating theatre.

Now, I have seen the insides of hospitals and worked in several, but all many years ago so no doubt am a bit behind the times on the latest inventions; but when I looked around me I felt that I had been brought into a television studio set for a *Dr Who* sequence! The machines dotted around were awe-inspiring enough, but when the doctor and her assistants began to don garments of some synthetic navy blue material in overall style, they looked like characters out of a science fiction film.

I was given a local anaesthetic for the operation, and would have liked to watch what the doctor was doing but things were so arranged that I just could not see. Wires were inserted into my left arm to reach down to the pulse in my wrist. A huge x-ray machine was above me, and again I was disappointed at not being able to see what was showing on the screen beyond it.

At last the doctor finished with me and I was taken to a ward which seemed to be bristling with more modern machines of every description, each one bigger and better that the last one I had seen.

The ward was glass-walled on two sides; a third side was one enormous picture window overlooking the town, and beyond the sea. From my bed I could see across a corridor into an open office with a ward beyond. At a long desk in the office sat people in attendance on the various electronic devices which were keeping checks on the recording gadgets to which I — and other patients — were individually connected. I now had strapped to my arm a temporary pacemaker which was attached to the wires in the arm, and also connected to a small TV screen which showed by little dots how my heart was beating.

On the other side of me was another, larger, machine. I was connected to this by some stickers on my chest which held the leads from the machine, the last — I was told — was recording my respirations; if one of these leads became disconnected, it made a bleeping noise which brought a Sister to fix it. This did not happen very often as generally I seemed to be satisfactorily firing on all cylinders.

I came to the conclusion during my stay there that nowadays nurses have to be not only ministering angels, but qualified electricians too. They were just wonderful in the way they carried out their duties, and ever cheerful and kindly.

Highly interested in the life of the busy hospital around me, my days passed very quickly. I made good progress with the temporary pacemaker, and the day came when I was taken to St George's Hospital in London to have a permanent one fitted. I travelled in a new cardiac unit ambulance, and again was attached to a machine and monitored all the way. The care and attention en route could not have been more had I been paying thousands of pounds for it instead of getting it all free on the National Health Service.

I had a local anaesthetic for the operation, which was to be on the right side. The one thing I was rather dreading was the withdrawing of the wires in the left arm which I knew was to be done. As with the previous operation, a large x-ray machine was in position, and a running commentary went on between two of the doctors as the work progressed. I was periodically called upon to co-operate: "Take a deep breath and hold it". "Cough!" "Pant like a dog." Eventually the pacemaker was in place and I was duly stitched. (The entry spot was in the chest just below the shoulder.) As to the removal of the wires of the temporary pacemaker, I never even felt them. The only discomfort throughout was the hardness of the operating table. I spent a week in the London hospital, feeling better every day, before being returned to my local hospital, after which I came home and find I can live a fairly normal life. I can no longer attend to my garden which I regret, but am content to live quietly and thankfully for the kindness and skill which has given me this new lease of life.

I am not even aware of the marvellous little object which has given me such relief, although I have to pay my respects to it each morning by checking my pulse rate. I have been given a margin either way by which it can safely vary. Should it exceed or drop below these limits, I have a phone number to resort to. Also, I have to go periodically for a check-up. Now, having reached my eightieth year, I am glad to be able to say that as yet my pacemaker has not needed any adjustment.

I belong to a club for the elderly where I still play bridge several times a week. I also spend many happy hours writing and working out word puzzles run by a magazine *Games and Puzzles*, although I haven't yet won a prize (except for a beautiful dictionary for writing a letter to the magazine saying how much I enjoyed the puzzles!).

So, with grandchildren and great grandchildren and so many interests, my life is still very full and happy.

★   ★   ★

Two months after writing the above lines, my Mother suffered a severe stroke from which she never recovered. In the nursing home one day, during one of her lucid moments, she told us, "I'm going to write an article about this experience. I think I could make it quite interesting."

So she could, with her sharp observation, and her eye always looking for the funny side of things; but God had other plans for her — the greatest Experience of all.

CHAPTER
SEVEN

Poems and Letters

by daughter, Barbara Anslow

IN MEMORY OF MRS VI EVANS
A popular entertainer on the Stanley Stage who died in
1942

(What she might have said at her own Funeral)

Well I'll be blowed! What, all these people, come to see
me put away?
Left their queues, and chores, and cooking?
(And it's such a nasty day —
Not a day you'd do your washing,
Never get it dry for weeks;
Yet what can you do when you have
Just two pair of flour-bag breeks?)

Why've you all got hankies with you?
That's what I should like to know!
(Big ones, too! That means more washing:
How that Welfare soap does go!)
Look here, don't tell me you're crying,

Weeping for the likes of me!
Goodness gracious! Well I never!
I don't call that tragedy.

After all, I'm no spring chicken
(Though I'm game for lots more fun);
There's younger folk than me been taken —
Fair's fair, when all's said and done.
I've had my youth, and then a husband
(Nicest chap you'd ever meet);
Yes, we lost our little girl — but
While we had her, she was sweet.

It's this crowd I can't get over —
Half of Stanley must have come!
Still, I s'pose it makes a change, a
Funeral breaks the old hum-drum.
Well, I think it's time you're moving
Back to work, and laugh, and chat;
And listen ! Don't waste time on crying
Over me: I'm gone — that's that!

HOME THOUGHTS FROM AN INTERNMENT CAMP

Is there really an England, I wonder?
Or is memory confused with a dream?
Was there ever a life without trouble or strife,
Where a lazy content reigned supreme?

Does there still stand a road trim with houses
All alike, yet a difference one?
(Nothing frightfully great, just the creak of a gate
That's a welcome when roaming is done.)

Did I ever rush to a hot kitchen
On a raw winter's late afternoon?
And toast hunks of bread that I afterwards spread
Thick with butter that melted too soon?

Was I once in a small old-world garden
Bright with roses and pansies and all?
And away at the end, a few Wyandottes penned,
And a cat sat in state on the wall.

There are none who can steal my illusions,
That is, if illusions they be;
And though all else may go, I have something no foe
Can appropriate — my memory.

OFF LIVERPOOL, OCTOBER 1945

I woke at six; expectant, thrilled.
The ship's pulsating heart was stilled.
I leapt out from my bunk, bright-eyed
And wrenched the porthole open wide.
In swept a rush of icy air;
I shivered, yet could only stare
Enraptured, at an English sea
With gray waves dancing angrily,
And interlaced with spitting foam.
Beyond were stretched dim hills of Home
Beneath a sky wind-racked and dull;
And as I gazed, a lonely gull
Swooped by, a smooth white rhapsody,
And screamed a welcome in at me.

(When the Japanese surrendered and the British Navy arrived in Hong Kong, the majority of the internees — including Mabel and I — had to remain in Stanley Camp awaiting ships to repatriate them to UK. The Hong Kong Police and many civil servants — including Olive and Barbara — were taken into the city to work with the temporary British administration. The two girls sent us almost daily reports of their new life in liberated Hong Kong, as the following extracts show.)

30th August 1945 7pm

Just a line to say I've arrived safely. Mrs R's two boys were very kind and deposited me and my luggage in French Mission on Battery Path. The Navy were already in the Dockyard Barracks as we came by. They were throwing cigs to the Chinese and waved to us. The Chinese were very excited. Nancy, Barbara B, Mrs M and self are in a room with wooden floor, wardrobe and 2 lovely armchairs it's luxury absolutely! We are dining in a few moments.

I think our flat might just about not have been bombed — the end flats were down, but only the top two floors of the block further down Gap Road. It was a great moment, seeing the Fleet lying in the harbour. I have seen a "Men Only" dated July 1945 (but only the outside so far, tho hope to see the inside later).

31st August 9.30am

I'm just taking the opportunity to snatch a few minutes to write when I can. There's heaps of work to do. I've been dished out with two lovely new pencils, unlimited stationery, carbons etc. — it's heavenly. The only thing like Stanley is that we have to queue for the bathroom.

Planes are still roaring overhead. Last night was just like coming to Calamba after Fort McKinley — flowers on the table, nice easy chairs with arms, boys to serve us; no sign of rice. Later, we lounged in front of the wireless set and heard Charles Moorod broadcasting about the "poor internees with sunken eyes"! — did you hear it?

Don't get worried about the reports in the newspaper of trouble — we haven't heard anything of it, and we're very near the Naval Yard; in any case, you won't catch me going downtown without an armed escort.

Breakfast this morning was the real thing — we nonchalantly read the daily paper while waiting to be served. Who said that congee tasts like porridge? I honestly didn't recognise porridge when it appeared, the taste is altogether different from what I expected, with milk and sugar ad lib; we also had pineapple, then a fried corned beef cake, with a few chips; there was bread and butter and jam ad lib, but I'm going easy on everything, because I don't want to upset my tummy and be sent back to Stanley! Being served is wonderful — there are boys even to light one's cigarette, if one smoked; I almost wished I did just for the luxury of being thus waited on.

A boy has just come round (it's about 11) serving coffee, but all I fancy is a drink of water, as I'm getting up an appetite for lunch. We can have tea and cake in the afternoon, and dinner is between 7 and 8.

264

I'm thoroughly enjoying myself but am somewhat in difficulties as my pants still haven't dried, and Nancy couldn't get me any when she went shopping this morning as all the big stores are closed. I won't sign for anything except absolute necessities, which are only pants at this moment.

The Japanese gendarmes are still keeping law and order, Nancy says. I'm content to take her word for it. We are quite safe here, and sleep on the very top floor of the French Mission. The fan is going in the office, and it just seems as if we've never had to shift for things the way we did at Stanley. It's a great experience here, and the luxuries of meals are just too too lovely — last night, when first sat down to dinner, I was almost afraid to take the first spoonful of creamed asparagus soup (complete with crackly toasted bread bits inside) because that is usually the stage in dreams at which one wakes up. Will you believe it, I couldn't even touch the sweet, which was pineapple on pastry, and my coffee I couldn't finish because it was too sweet altogether.

Had you forgotten that cups of tea and coffee usually sit in saucers? I had! And honestly, I couldn't think what to do with a serviette when I saw one sitting on the table in front of me. I looked at it once, then remembered "Oh, a serviette" I automatically put it on my lap, but it didn't look right somehow; this is the real truth, I'm not trying to be funny. I remembered they were sometimes tucked down our dresses and worn that way, but I just couldn't see what good the thing was going to do on my lap; it was only the size of a pocket hanky; anyway, having put it on my lap, I didn't

265

dare move for fear of drawing public attention to myself, and breathed a sigh of relief when I saw other people doing the same. I felt such a fool!

31st August, later.

Tonight and at tiffin time we had peanuts on plates to nibble between meals — only about Military Yen 1,000 worth every two yards down the two long tables!

Just this minute received your note, and glad the party was a success. I do envy you having that talk to the naval person, though I feel heartily sorry for him — I bet he didn't know which of you to answer first. I imagine you have no voice left at all this morning.

I hope we do all go to Australia, as you suggest, but haven't really much hopes that Olive and I will get away with the rest of you. Anyway, maybe we won't be very long after you. So funny to hear trams groaning past, and dogs barking etc. But the best sight of all is the fleet anchored out in the stream.

Hope you received my sugar ration all right. Mabel was quite right — I don't need my plate and spoon and mug and will try to send them in to you. This morning I glimpsed one of the Fathers in this building — had heard they weren't here, but maybe they were only visiting. Mr MacFadyen is in town so when I see him I'm going to ask him about Sunday Mass, and if we can get away from work, will ask him to take me to St Joseph's, but don't worry that I'll go through fire and smoke or do anything foolish, because I'm much too keen to see the end of this business, having existed so long.

Planes are zooming over us all day long — I wonder they haven't got tired of it — I have. Any sign of the parachute goods yet? I'm working in particular for Mr Megarry, but we are all apt to have any work shot at us by anyone who comes in.

2pm. Just back from tiffin — consommé, white bread, thick meat stew with English potato (as I was rather late, got shortish rations of potatoes); then a slice of pineapple with syrup over it and a helping of junket. There were also bowls of peanuts on the table, but I didn't have time to stay and nibble many. All very delicious. Are you getting anything more interesting than meat yet?

Did I leave the nut from my camp bed at home?[1] One is missing — it's the bit that goes on the end of the screw securing the legs. If you find it, perhaps you'd send it.

I learned that the Hospital ship is leaving tomorrow and I'm all agog to know whether you and Mabel are to go too. We don't seem to have any information as to whether it is only a very short list that are leaving tomorrow, and we can't ring Stanley unless they ring us, so I'm hoping Stanley will ring up and we can ask for details.

Things are happening so quickly that one hardly has time to think. It's really too much to take in that people really are sailing away at last. Let me know what you're putting down to do in the event of any choice of going or staying, won't you, so I shall know what to do too.

---

[1] "home" = our room in Stanley!

1st September

I've just come back from a shopping expedition. The only thing I bought was a tin of Dutch Baby milk which I'll be sending you either tonight or tomorrow, it cost 100 Yen. I was given that as an advance, and it won't buy anything I really need, like pants. Actually, I think I can manage for clothes, as someone said we were assured that plenty of clothes will be arriving, women's underwear included. We went into the Asia Company[1] which hasn't very much stock, it is mostly a restaurant now. They will let us sign for anything.

While in the Asia Company a voice hailed us and seated at a table were Mr Allan, Mr Ebbage and two friends. They made us sit down with them, and we had ICE-CREAM! It was delicious; then a glass of cider, complete with gas. Mr Allan is moving in to the Dockyard tomorrow and has promised to scrounge me some magazines. I'm dying to see photos of Shirley and Deanna etc.

Did you get the chocolate we sent all right? And if so, wasn't it nice? The funny thing about town is the lack of traffic, especially buses; a few stray crackers are being let off from time to time; not many people about, but quite a number of troops, ex pows and otherwise.

Three of the Nurses off the Hospital ship had dinner with us, and were very interested to know how we had been treated. They looked so fresh and well-covered.

---

[1] The Asia Company supplied us with groceries before the war.

PS Send replies in the big envelope I sent you — we can use it for some time then.

4th September a.m.

I sent you yesterday, one tin of butter by Mr W (and two pieces of bread), then two small loaves of bread and a slab of chocolate by George Watt.

Well, like Barbara, I am glad I came. Stanley seems like another life now. Rene Razavette and I have a nice large room on the 4th floor of the Gloucester Hotel and a lovely bed each. I just died in bed last night. You might wash my two sheets sometime and send them me, but no hurry as I have borrowed one.

The meals are very good, I wish I could send some of them in to you. Now we are here I don't mind if we have to stay on for a while. Everything seems quite normal around the town. I'm surprised at the stocks of food the little shops have. I will get some more stuff if possible to send in.

We have been given forms on which you have to state if you have signed any sterling cheques. I will send it to you because you signed that one, and perhaps there might not be enough forms to go round in Stanley. By the numbers of men around here there can't be many left in Stanley. I met Mr Tribble yesterday and he had been to the cemetery and up to Dad's grave. He said it was all in good order, except for a couple of turfs which had fallen on it and which he had removed. They were very likely from the landslide which I hear is somewhere on Stubbs Road.

The "Oxfordshire" went yesterday, though we didn't actually see it leave. I'm in the same office as Barbara at the moment in the Hong Kong & Shanghai Bank (before, her office was in the French Mission). We eat at the Hong Kong Hotel, and the curfew is at nine. We don't have to go out to get from the Gloucester to the Hong Kong Hotel, as we go through the Arcade.

I hope your food at Stanley is improving. I suppose you will all be settling down again to bridge now all the excitement is over for a time. Don't go overdoing it in any way.

4th September

Thanks very much for the shoes, film book and specs. Olive and I went out shopping yesterday after 5 and treated ourselves to an ice-cream and cider, but won't be too extravagant — that was just a first fling. I don't mind telling you all these galling details because I'm sure you two will get on an early ship and enjoy even more luxuries than ourselves.

We know nothing about repatriation or evacuation here, but we're anxious to know what is happening about you two. If you are to go soon, we may be able to get in to see you, and in any case will have to collect the remainder of our luggage. We hope that you will be able to send us a skirt each or something that can be made into a skirt as clothes are going to be a problem. Thanks very much for the much needed pants. How about trying to get that other dress out of Mrs R — the dark one she wanted to swop? If she is going away soon, she may not want it.

270

Hope you enjoyed the bread and butter and choc. we sent. Olive and I have decided to draw a certain sum of Yen each and buy stuff right away to send to you. But we will keep our horns well in — don't worry, we won't buy anything but food, and not much of that. I can get you a jar of pickles for 50 Yen: not from the Asia Company though, will have to wait for cash and buy them from some other shop.

Both Olive and I are coatless — what happens in wet weather I don't know. If one of us gets a trip in to Stanley in the near future, we will bring back Peggy's mosquito net (which I don't need, living on the top floor is all right, haven't seen one mosquito there so far), and can collect a coat for each of us. It's too much to ask any one to transport such bulky things.

Things are rapidly becoming organised, but most of the men are pretty tired, working very hard, with very little rest, and so many of them aren't fit to do so. Three weeks ago, we would never have believed it possible to do so much in present conditions. For myself, I'm feeling in fine fettle, and just beginning to settle down enough to want to have something to do in the evenings after work. I have some German with me, and a poetry book. Judging by my white skirt, I think I've put on a little weight. Work agrees with me, and things aren't nearly so hectic as in the new offices, as we have a typists' room to ourselves, with only one telephone, whereas in the French Mission a large number of staff shared one big room, and we were always having to answer the phones and chase up and down stairs trying to find people we didn't know.

We see from today's paper that Stanley isn't faring too well. Never mind. I expect things will improve in due course. Our meals have been slightly more substantial these last few days, though we're getting blasé enough to say "corned beef again!" as if it was rice and stew!

The Chinese are still celebrating with fire-crackers; more and more shops are getting ready to open, by sticking a cardboard notice on their shutters or in the window, with their name. It's intriguing to see things becoming more and more normal every day.

Still haven't had a hot bath, and our ambition is to dine on one of the ships and see their movies; quite a lot of the men have done this.

I enclose a piece of paper for reply — don't use it for bridge scores!

ISIS publish a wide range of books in large print, from fiction to biography. Any suggestions for books you would like to see in large print or audio are always welcome. Please send to the Editorial department at:

ISIS Publishing Ltd.
7 Centremead
Osney Mead
Oxford OX2 0ES
(01865) 250 333

A full list of titles is available free of charge from:
Ulverscroft large print books

(UK)
The Green
Bradgate Road, Anstey
Leicester LE7 7FU
Tel: (0116) 236 4325

(Australia)
P.O Box 953
Crows Nest
NSW 1585
Tel: (02) 9436 2622

(USA)
1881 Ridge Road
P.O Box 1230, West Seneca,
N.Y. 14224-1230
Tel: (716) 674 4270

(Canada)
P.O Box 80038
Burlington
Ontario L7L 6B1
Tel: (905) 637 8734

(New Zealand)
P.O Box 456
Feilding
Tel: (06) 323 6828

Details of **ISIS** complete and unabridged audio books are also available from these offices. Alternatively, contact your local library for details of their collection of **ISIS** large print and unabridged audio books.